Penitential Services

OLIVER CRILLY

PENITENTIAL SERVICES

the columba press

the columba press

8 Lr Kilmacud Road, Blackrock, Co Dublin, Ireland

First edition 1986
Cover by Bill Bolger
Typeset by
Printset & Design Ltd
Printed in Ireland by
Mount Salus Press

Imprimatur
✠ Edward Daly
Bishop of Derry
February 1986

ISBN 0 948183 12 8

Quotations from the Good News Bible are used by permission of the Bible Societies. Psalms are used by permission of The Grail England. The blessing in Irish on page 121 is used by permission of the Irish Episcopal Commission on the Liturgy. The quotation from *Be not afraid* by Jean Vanier, is used by permission of Gill & Macmillan. The prayers from *The Children of God Series* are used by permission of Veritas Publications.

CONTENTS

INTRODUCTION

Reflecting on the forgiveness of Mehmet Ali Agca by Pope John Paul II, *Time* magazine quoted John Dryden's: "Forgiveness to the injured doth belong". Deeds are done by individuals, said the *Time* writer, and must be judged individually. There is a sense in which that represents a part of the Church's understanding of her own discipline of reconciliation. The individual must seek forgiveness; the acts of the penitent are an essential part of the celebration of the sacrament of reconciliation:

> "Reconciliation of individual penitents is the only normal and ordinary way of celebrating the sacrament." (*Reconciliatio et Paenitentia*, paragraph 32.)

The Church's tradition of reconciliation goes far beyond the one to one confrontation indicated by the magazine writer, of course. In the understanding of the Church, reconciliation has been achieved by the sacrifice of Christ, and all reconciliation in the Church's daily practice is rooted in Christ's reconciliation:

> "All this is from God, who through Christ reconciled us to himself and gave us the ministry of reconciliation" (2 Cor 5:18).

In the new "Rite of Penance", the Church envisages, as well as the ordinary one to one celebration of the sacrament, a communal celebration concluding with individual confession and absolution (Rite 2), and in very exceptional and carefully regulated circumstances general confession and absolution (Rite 3). Rite 2 is considered as just as normal a celebration as Rite 1:

> "The second form — reconciliation of a number of penitents with individual confession and absolution — even though in the preparatory acts it helps to give greater emphasis to the community aspects of the sacrament, is the same as the first form in the culminating sacramental act, namely, individual confession and individual absolution of sins. It can thus be regarded as equal to

the first form as regards the normality of the rite" (*Reconciliatio et Paenitentia*, paragraph 32.)

What the Apostolic Exhortation calls "the community aspects of the sacrament" have received greater expression in pastoral practice in recent years, and the need for resource material for communal celebrations has increased. That is one reason for the present publication, which makes no claim either to be exhaustive or to impose its outline celebrations rigidly. It is more like a quarry from which people may draw away the blocks which suit their purposes in order to build up the particular celebration which corresponds to the pastoral needs of their own place and time. If a celebrant finds that a complete outline fills his need on a given occasion, and he is saved some time and energy in researching further, that is a bonus, and we will be glad to have been of assistance.

There is one other aspect of these penitential celebrations that may be worth reflecting on. They offer the opportunity to small groups, perhaps even families, and to larger parish groups to reflect prayerfully on our continuing need for forgiveness and for healing and reconciliation. In this context, many of the celebrations need not necessarily end with sacramental confession and absolution. Something like the penitential rite at Mass might very well suffice on a particular occasion, leaving the participants to seek sacramental reconciliation later in their own time. Whether there is sacramental confession or not, the emphasis on the ongoing need for forgiveness is a valuable part of what takes place — a call to conversion and a reassurance of God's faithful love and faithful forgiveness.

A priest might also consider it useful, from time to time, to use some of these outlines, or part of some of them, as an aid to preparation for confession, just before the ordinary Saturday confessions in the Parish.

Dr. Haddon Willmer has written and lectured a good deal on "the politics of forgiveness". He is referring not only to the need for forgiveness in the political arena, as in the north of Ireland, but to our need to locate the experience of forgiveness in the reality of our daily lives, rather than lock it away in a ritual remoteness. Forgiveness is accepting the limitations of ourselves, of those around us, of the situation in which we find ourselves.

Forgiveness is difficult. Yet every time we seek forgiveness we are called to forgive each other, to see each other today without the burden of yesterday's grudges, to get up today without yesterday's anger. Forgiveness is difficult, just as genuine love is difficult, because it is unconditional. Chiara Lubich has a beautiful phrase for it: she has referred to forgiveness as "amnesty in the heart": . . . "forgiving seventy times seven, drawing close to all with this complete amnesty in the heart, with this universal forgiveness" (*New City* magazine). We need to provide more occasions where people can reflect, prayerfully and under the guidance of the word of God in the Scriptures, on the need for this ongoing forgiveness in our lives, and on the generosity with which God offers us healing and reconciliation. Gathered together in this book is the written summary of how some people have tried to structure simple occasions of reflection and of celebration when we invite God's healing and forgiving love into our lives. We hope they will prove useful.

Oliver Crilly
Lá 'le Bríde 1986

OUTLINE STRUCTURE OF PENITENTIAL SERVICES

Some of the services in this book are sacramental and some of them are intended just as a prayerful reflection on forgiveness and reconciliation, perhaps with some symbolic content, and perhaps concluding with a simple prayer for forgiveness, like the Penitential Rite from the beginning of the Mass. It is not necessary to fit them all into one category, or to envisage only one unchanging structure for them. However, for the sacramental penitential services which correspond to Rite 2 of the new Rite of Penance, a basic structure is given in the Introduction to the New Rite. A summary appears below. Further details may be checked by reference to the text of the new Rite of Penance itself. The Rite also contains a variety of suitable texts which would enrich any service.

Summary of Structure

Introductory Rites

> Entrance Hymn
> Sign of the Cross
> Greeting
> Introduction
> Opening Prayer

Celebration of the word of God

> Scripture Readings
> Homily
> Examination of Conscience

Liturgy of Reconciliation

> Form of General Confession (eg. Confiteor)
> Litany or Song (of contrition, forgiveness, God's mercy)
> The Our Father (which is never omitted)
> Individual Confession and Absolution

Exhortation (to thanksgiving and good works)
Praise for God's Mercy (psalm, hymn, litany, e.g. Magnificat)
Concluding Prayer of Thanksgiving

Concluding Rite
Blessing
Dismissal

ADVENT I

Oliver Crilly

Theme: Towards the coming of the Lord

Opening hymn and enthronement of the Book

As the opening hymn is sung, the President, Readers, Homilist, Confessors and Servers enter in procession with the Lectionary, solemnly enthrone it on the lectern and the President incenses it.

P In the name of the Father, and of the Son, and of the Holy Spirit.

℟ Amen.

P The grace of our Lord Jesus Christ
   and the love of God
   and the fellowship of the Holy Spirit
   be with you all.

℟ And also with you.

P Let us pray to God our Father
   that we may sincerely call to mind our sins
   as we wait in joyful hope
   for the coming of our Saviour Jesus Christ.

Pause for silent prayer.

P All praise to you, almighty Father,
fountain of all holiness.
You so loved the world
that you sent your only Son
that we might know your will
for our salvation.
Help us to live in faith and love
as we wait in hope till he comes again.

We ask this through Jesus Christ our Lord.

℟ Amen.

THE LITURGY OF THE WORD

First Reading   Tit 2:11-14

A reading from the letter of St Paul to Titus.

God has revealed his grace for the salvation of all mankind. That grace instructs us to give up ungodly living and worldly passions, and to live self-controlled, upright, and godly lives in this world, as we wait for the blessed day we hope for, when the glory of our great God and Saviour Jesus Christ will appear. He gave himself for us, to rescue us from all wickedness and to make us a pure people who belong to him alone and are eager to do good.

This is the word of the Lord.

℞ Thanks be to God.

Second Reading   Pet 1:3, 4, 6, 7

A reading from the first letter of St Peter.

Let us give thanks to the God and Father of our Lord Jesus Christ! Because of his great mercy he gave us new life by raising Jesus Christ from death. This fills us with a living hope, and so we look forward to possessing the rich blessings that God keeps for his people.

Be glad about this, even though it may now be necessary for you to be sad for a while because of the many kinds of trials you suffer. Their purpose is to prove that your faith is genuine. Even gold, which can be destroyed, is tested by fire; and so your faith, which is much more precious than gold, must also be tested, so that it may endure. Then you will receive praise and glory and honour on the day when Jesus Christ is revealed.

This is the word of the Lord.

℞ Thanks be to God.

A short period of silence follows, for personal reflection.

Gospel Reading   Mt 25:31-40

A reading from the holy Gospel according to Matthew.

"When the Son of Man comes as King and all the angels with him, he will sit on his royal throne, and the people of all the nations will be gathered before him. Then he will divide them into two groups, just as a shepherd separates the sheep from the goats. He will put the righteous people on his right and the others on his left. Then the King will say to the people on his right, 'Come, you that are blessed by my Father! Come and possess the kingdom which has been prepared for you ever since the creation of the world. I was hungry and you fed me, thirsty and you gave me a drink; I was a stranger and you received me in your homes, naked and you clothed me; I was sick and you took care of me, in prison and you visited me.'

The righteous will then answer him, 'When, Lord, did we ever see you hungry and feed you, or thirsty and give you a drink? When did we ever see you a stranger and welcome you in our homes, or naked and clothe you? When did we ever see you sick or in prison, and visit you?' The King will reply, 'I tell you, whenever you did this for one of the least important of these brothers of mine, you did it for me!'

This is the Gospel of the Lord.

℞ Praise to you, Lord Jesus Christ.

Homily
The homily leads onto an examination of conscience and is followed by a period of silence for personal reflection.

THE SACRAMENT OF PENANCE

My brothers and sisters, confess your sins and pray for each other, that you may be healed.

All: I confess to almighty God,
and to you, my brothers and sisters,
that I have sinned through my own fault
in my thoughts and in my words,
in what I have done,
and in what I have failed to do;
and I ask blessed Mary, every virgin,
all the angels and saints,
and you, my brothers and sisters,
to pray for me to the Lord our God.

P Let us now pray to the Father in the words our Saviour gave us:
Our Father . . .

Sign of Peace
P As brothers and sisters in Christ,
reconciled with one another before God,
let us offer each other a sign of peace.

Individual Confession
Reflective music may be played during individual confession, with adequate periods of prayerful silence. There should be enough priests available to conclude the confessions in a reasonable time, but if numbers for confession are very large, the final prayer and blessing may be said after a fixed period, with confessions continuing afterwards for the rest of the congregation.

Praise of God's Mercy
All things are done according to God's plan and decision; and God chose us to be his own people in union with Christ because of his own purpose, based on what he had decided from the very beginning.

Let us, then, who were the first to hope in Christ, praise God's glory!

And you also became God's people when you heard the true message, the Good News that brought you salvation.

You believed in Christ, and God put his stamp of ownership on you by giving you the Holy Spirit he had promised.

The Spirit is the guarantee that we shall receive what God has promised his people, and this assures us that God will give complete freedom to those who are his.

Let us praise his glory!

Eph 1:3-14

Final Prayer
P All thanks and praise to you, almighty Father,
God of compassion and mercy.

May we who have again received your endless mercy
and forgiveness,
go out from here now
to show your love and compassion
to all those we meet
that the world may know the glory of your Son.

We ask this through Christ our Lord.

℟ Amen.

Blessing

P May almighty God bless you,
the Father, and the Son, ✠ and the Holy Spirit.

℟ Amen.

Dismissal

P Go in peace to love and serve the Lord.

℟ Thanks be to God.

ADVENT II
Jack McArdle, SS CC

Note: Parts I, II and III should be limited to five minutes each.

I Gospel Reading   Jn 1:15-39
A reading from the holy Gospel according to John.

John spoke about him. He cried out, "This is the one I was talking about when I said, 'He comes after me, but he is greater than I am, because he existed before I was born.' "

Out of the fullness of his grace he has blessed us all, giving us one blessing after another. God gave the Law through Moses, but grace and truth came through Jesus Christ. No one has ever seen God. The only Son, who is the same as God and is at the Father's side, he has made him known.

The Jewish authorities in Jerusalem sent some priests and Levites to John, to ask him, "Who are you?"

John did not refuse to answer, but spoke out openly and clearly, saying: "I am not the Messiah."

"Who are you, then?" they asked. "Are you Elijah?"

"No," he replied.

"Then tell us who you are," they said. "We have to take an answer back to those who sent us. What do you say about yourself?"

John answered by quoting the prophet Isaiah:

"I am 'the voice of someone shouting in the desert: Make a straight path for the Lord to travel!' "

The messengers, who had been sent by the Pharisees, then asked John, "If you are not the Messiah nor Elijah nor the Prophet, why do you baptise?"

John answered "I baptise with water, but among you stands the one you do not know. He is coming after me, but I am not good enough even to untie his sandals."

All this happened in Bethany on the east side of the River Jordan, where John was baptising.

The next day John saw Jesus coming to him, and said, "There is the Lamb of God, who takes away the sin of the world! This is the one I was talking about when I said, 'A man is coming after me, but he is greater than I am, because he existed before I was born.' I did not know who he would be, but I came baptising with water in order to make him known to the people of Israel."

And John gave this testimony: "I saw the Spirit come down like a dove from heaven and stay on him. I still did not know that he was the one, but God, who sent me to baptise with water, had said to me, 'You will see the Spirit come down, and stay on a man; he is the one who baptises with the Holy Spirit.'

"I have seen it," said John, "and I tell you that he is the Son of God."

The next day John was standing there again with two of his disciples, when he saw Jesus walking by. "There is the Lamb of God!" he said.

The two disciples heard him say this and went with Jesus. Jesus turned, saw them following him, and asked, "What are you looking for?"

They answered, "Where do you live, Rabbi?" (This word means "Teacher.")

"Come and see," he answered. (It was then about four o'clock in the afternoon.) So they went with him and saw where he lived, and spent the rest of that day with him.

This is the Gospel of the Lord.

℟ Praise to you, Lord Jesus Christ.

Reflection

Preparing the manger of our hearts for the coming of Jesus. Listening to John the Baptist calling on us to prepare the way of the Lord, to make straight his path. Asking the Spirit of God to switch on the full beam of his light in our hearts — to show up and reveal the sins, the flaws, the hurts, the resentments, the weaknesses that make my heart and soul an unfit place for God to dwell.

Pause for quiet meditation — to a quiet version of "Prepare ye the Way of the Lord."

II Gospel Reading   Lk 2:1-7

A reading from the holy Gospel according to Luke.

At that time the Emperor Augustus ordered a census to be taken throughout the Roman Empire. When this first census took place, Quirinius was the governor of Syria. Everyone, then, went to register himself, each to his own town.

Joseph went from the town of Nazareth in Galilee to the town of Bethlehem in Judaea, the birthplace of King David. Joseph went there because he was a descendant of David. He went to register with Mary, who was promised in marriage to him. She was pregnant, and while they were in Bethlehem, the time came for her to have her baby. She gave birth to her first son, wrapped him in strips of cloth and laid him in a manger — there was no room for them to stay in the inn.

This is the Gospel of the Lord.

℟ Praise to you, Lord Jesus Christ.

Reflection

There was no room for him — many people just didn't want to know. They had no time. They couldn't be bothered. At least they had some excuse — they just didn't know. Even on the cross Jesus would ask the Father to forgive those who were killing him — because they didn't know either.

We certainly cannot claim that excuse. What a tragedy if, 2000 years later, we still have no time, couldn't be bothered, just don't want to know. Until such time as we throw open the doors of our hearts and souls and invite Jesus to come and live there — until that time, we cannot have any meaning or any sincerity in celebrating Christmas. What would Jesus discover in your heart if you opened the doors now and invited him in?

Pause for reflection with quiet 'mood' music.

III Gospel Reading   Jn 1:10-13

A reading from the holy Gospel according to John.

The Word was in the world, and though God made the world through him, yet the world did not recognise him. He came to his own country, but his own people did not receive him. Some, however, did receive him and believed in him; so he gave them the right to become God's children. They did not become God's children by natural means, that is, by being born as the children of a human father; God himself was their Father.

This is the Gospel of the Lord.

℟ Praise to you, Lord Jesus Christ.

Reflection

"He came unto his own and his own received him not. But to those who did receive him he gave the right to become children of God." He came as a Saviour and Redeemer — and he came to forgive sinners and to free slaves to sin. He invited us into the family, children of God, able to call God Father, Abba, Daddy.

Christmas is a time for home-coming. If we can at all we all like to be with our families at Christmas. Even the day after Christmas is often spent visiting our extended family — grandparents, cousins, and so on.

Jesus is inviting you home for Christmas. You may be a real Prodigal, but he assures you of the Father's hug. Come to Jesus now and tell him that you want to come home, that you want to start again. Let this be a real Christmas, when like a poor shepherd who has just been told the Good News, you run to Bethlehem to kneel at a manger, to welcome a Saviour. You may have longed for such an event, for such a coming. That is nothing compared to the intense longing in the heart of Jesus for you to come to him. Now there's joy in heaven — the sinner and the Saviour are meeting.

Music: "Angels we have heard on high."

20

IV   Individual Celebration of the Sacrament

Those coming forward to celebrate the Sacrament could be encouraged to begin in one of the following ways:

1. *"I want to come home to God's family for Christmas, because I have wandered away when I . . ."*

2. *"I wish to invite Jesus into the stable of my heart and soul, and I ask his forgiveness and his freedom from bondage because of what he finds there . . ."*

3. *"In this time of Advent, I, too, want to begin all over again, because I . . ."*

Suggestion: As people go forward for the Sacrament, there is a need for a person at the mike, to help maintain an atmosphere of prayer and of prayerful quiet. An occasional short prayer, a little reminder of what's happening, and appropriate music for a prayerful atmosphere.

Just keep things flowing gently, and with an atmosphere of warmth and love.

V   Conclusion

Ideal if all ministers of the Sacrament had gathered around the altar at the beginning, as the Blessed Sacrament was exposed. Then at end of Part III they go to their places of ministry (or of "welcome"?). At the end of the Service they return to the altar for a communal prayer of penance, a final blessing and dismissal.

LENT I

Brian Magee, CM

Opening Hymn
Music should be chosen to suit the congregation. Additional hymns and psalms may be used in other parts of the service at choice.

Introduction
The priest greets the congregation:
Grace, mercy, and peace be with you from God the Father and Christ Jesus our Saviour.
People: And also with you.

Celebrant
During this time of renewal we are called in a special way to remember our Baptism. This time of Lent is especially given to the celebration of Baptism. Throughout the Christian world many thousands are preparing to be baptised at Easter, and each of us is called to join with them by renewing our own baptism. We have first to remember our own baptism — something that is difficult for most of us because we were baptised as infants. But I remember through knowing what the sacrament should mean for me in my daily living now. In that remembering I come to know how I should be living as a Christian, and how far I am from that ideal. And renewal means repenting for my failure and resolving once more to live by the promises once made for me by my parents and godparents. Let us begin by prayer for that grace.

Prayer
Let us pray.
Lord our God, you have called us to be a chosen race, a royal priesthood, a consecrated nation, a people set apart. You have called us out of darkness into your wonderful light. We acknowledge that we have not lived up to our calling, but have sinned before you. Renew once more, through the tears of repentance, the grace that came to us in the water of baptism.
We ask this through Christ our Lord.   ℞ Amen.

First Reading

Introduction to reading.
Through our baptism we choose to serve the Lord, our God. Living our baptism means putting away all temptations to follow other gods.

First Reading   24:1-2, 15-15
A reading from the book of Joshua.

Joshua gathered all the tribes of Israel together at Shechem. He called the elders, the leaders, the judges, and the officers of Israel, and they came into the presence of God. Joshua said to all the people, "If you are not willing to serve him, decide today whom you will serve, the gods your ancestors worshipped in Mesopotamia or the gods of the Amorites, in whose land you are now living. As for my family and me, we will serve the Lord."

The people replied, "We would never leave the Lord to serve other gods! The Lord our God brought our fathers and us out of slavery in Egypt, and we saw the miracles that he performed. He kept us safe wherever we went among all the nations through which we passed. So we also will serve the Lord; he is our God."

Joshua said to the people, "But you may not be able to serve the Lord. He is a holy God and will not forgive your sins. He will tolerate no rivals, and if you leave him to serve foreign gods, he will turn against you and punish you. He will destroy you, even though he was good to you before."

The people said to Joshua, "No! We *will* serve the Lord."

Joshua said to them, "You are your own witnesses to the fact that you have chosen to serve the Lord."

"Yes," they said, "we are witnesses."

"Then get rid of those foreign gods that you have," he demanded, "and pledge your loyalty to the Lord, the God of Israel."

The people then said to Joshua, "We will serve the Lord our God. We will obey his commands."

So Joshua made a covenant for the people that day.

This is the word of the Lord.

℞ Thanks be to God.

Responsorial Psalm   Ps 125

RESPONSE: What marvels the Lord worked for us!
          Indeed we were glad.

1. When the Lord delivered Zion from bondage,
   it seemed like a dream.
   Then was our mouth filled with laughter,
   on our lips there were songs. ℞

2. The heathen themselves said: 'What marvels
   the Lord worked for them!'
   What marvels the Lord worked for us!
   Indeed we were glad. ℞

3. Deliver us, O Lord, from our bondage
   as streams in dry land.
   Those who are sowing in tears
   will sing when they reap. ℞

4. They go out, they go out, full of tears,
   carrying seed for the sowing:
   they come back, they come back, full of song,
   carrying their sheaves. ℞

Second Reading
Introduction to reading.

We are reborn into the family of God through baptism; we should
be no longer dead through sin.

Second Reading   Rom 6:3-4, 8-11
A reading from the letter of St Paul to the Romans.

For surely you know that when we were baptised into union with
Christ Jesus, we were baptised into union with his death. By our
baptism, then, we were buried with him and shared his death, in order
that, just as Christ was raised from death by the glorious power of
the Father, so also we might live a new life.

Since we have died with Christ, we believe that we will also live with
him. For we know that Christ has been raised from death and will

never die again — death will no longer rule over him. And so, because he died, sin has no power over him; and now he lives his life in fellowship with God. In the same way you are to think of yourselves as dead, so far as sin is concerned, but living in fellowship with God through Christ Jesus.

This is the word of the Lord.

℞ Thanks be to God.

Acclamation

Glory and praise to you, O Christ!
God loved the world so much
that he gave his only Son;
everyone who believes in him has eternal life.
Glory and praise to you, O Christ!

Gospel Reading   Jn 3:16-21
A reading from the holy Gospel according to John.

For God loved the world so much that he gave his only Son, so that everyone who believes in him may not die but have eternal life. For God did not send his Son into the world to be its judge, but to be its saviour.

Whoever believes in the Son is not judged; but whoever does not believe has already been judged, because he has not believed in God's only Son. This is how the judgement works: the light has come into the world, but people love the darkness rather than the light, because their deeds are evil. Anyone who does evil things hates the light and will not come to the light, because he does not want his evil deeds to be shown up. But whoever does what is true comes to the light in order that the light may show that what he did was in obedience to God.

This is the Gospel of the Lord.

℞ Praise to you, Lord Jesus Christ.

Homily

Just like the first Christians, most communities of believers live in a world that is mainly pagan. It is a world that does not understand the Christian way of living, and is often hostile to it. Those first Christians were often reminded that they should show their distinctiveness by a higher moral code. They were a people called to holiness through the baptism that had separated them from the unbeliever. St Clement reminded them that "we have to keep our baptism pure and undefiled". He was, of course, speaking to Christians who had gone through a long process of preparing for baptism. They were people who saw the difference between their present way of life and what they had been once. They had renounced Satan and sin, they had made solemn promises. They recognised that they were now dead to sin and alive to Jesus Christ. To fail through sin would be a great shame and be unexpected. In time the Christian community did have those who failed, those whom St Cyprian described as having "broken their oath to Christ".

But always the Church has recognised that receiving baptism means entering into a distinctive way of life which calls for rejecting sin and being committed to virtue.

One of the signs that Christians began a new life at Baptism was in the reclothing of the person who had gone down into the baptismal pool and been washed clean of the past life. The new white clothes given then symbolised a new person coming out of that font. St Paul refers to this when he says: 'You have stripped off your old behaviour with your old self and you have put on a new self.' The tradition of the white garment, or baptismal robe, stays with us. We all had the white garment placed on us while the priest said to each of us: "You have become a new creation, and have clothed yourself in Christ. See in this white garment the outward sign of your Christian dignity. With your family and friends to help you by word and example, bring that dignity unstained into the everlasting life of heaven."

We give a real meaning to our baptism when we try to live a sinless life. But more positively we find that real meaning in a life of Christian standards, when we live as Christ called us to, when we live as he lived.

The wish of the priest at the giving of the white garment significantly reminds us that we cannot do it alone. We belong to a community, we are baptised into a body. We are called to be members one of another, to live a life of love. We support each other by word and example; and we can fail each other in the same way.

And we do fail to live up to the Gospel standards. Our identity through baptism is as a follower of Christ and his way. We try as Lent comes round each year (or at our annual retreat) to recall ourselves to that standard, to confess our failures in the past, and to renew once more our baptismal promises. Let us now take time to look at the demands of the Gospel for us before we confess our failures.

Examination of Conscience

St Paul wrote to his new Christians at Colossae to remind them that being raised up with Christ they must live a life hidden with Christ in God. He spells out for them what it means to be dead to sin. Let us examine ourselves by his standards: (*Col. 3:5- 5:4*)

You must kill everything in you that is earthly: sexual vice, impurity, uncontrolled passion, evil desires.

Especially you must kill greed, which is the same thing as worshipping a false god.

You must give up human anger, hot temper, malice, abusive language and dirty talk.

You must not lie to each other.

You are to be clothed in heartfelt compassion, in generosity and humility, gentleness and patience.

You are to bear with one another; forgive each other if one of you has a complaint against another.

You are to let the Word of Christ, in all its richness, find a home with you.

You are to have gratitude in your hearts as you join with the Church in the worship of God.

Husbands and wives, you are to love one another and not be sharp with each other.

Children, you are to be obedient to your parents always, because that is what will please the Lord.

Parents, you are not to irritate your children, but encourage them or they will lose heart.

Employers, you are to make sure that those who work for you are given what is fair and upright.

Whatever your work is, you are to put your heart into it as done for the Lord.

You are to be persevering in your prayers and be thankful always.

Act of Repentance

My brothers and sisters, confess your sins and pray for each other, that you may be healed:

I confess to almighty God,
and to you, my brothers and sisters,
that I have sinned through my own fault
in my thoughts and in my words,
in what I have done,
and in what I have failed to do;
and I ask blessed Mary, ever virgin,
all the angels and saints,
and you, my brothers and sisters,
to pray for me to the Lord our God.

Renewal of Baptismal Promises

If in the pastoral judgement of the priest, it does not conflict with the celebration at the Easter Vigil, the Renewal of Baptismal Promises may take place now. The people may hold candles lighted from the Easter candle if that is convenient.

Celebrant: Through the Paschal mystery, dear friends, we are buried with Christ by Baptism into his death, and raised with him to newness of life. I call upon you, therefore, to renew the solemn promises and vows of Holy Baptism, by which you once renounced Satan and all his works, and promised to serve God faithfully in his holy Catholic Church.

Do you reaffirm your renunciation of evil and renew your commitment to Jesus Christ?

People: I do.

C Do you believe in God the Father almighty, creator of heaven and earth?

P I do.

C Do you believe in Jesus Christ his only Son our Lord, who was born of the Virgin Mary, was crucified, died, and was buried, rose from the dead, and is now seated at the right hand of the Father?

P I do.

C Do you believe in the Holy Spirit, the holy catholic Church, the communion of saints, the forgiveness of sins, the resurrection of the body, and life everlasting?

P I do.

C Will you continue in the apostles' teaching and fellowship, in the breaking of bread, and in the prayers?

P I will, with God's help.

C Will you persevere in resisting evil, and, whenever you fall into sin, repent and return to the Lord?

P I will, with God's help.

C Will you proclaim by word and example the Good News of God in Christ?

P I will, with God's help.

C Will you seek and serve Christ in all persons, loving your neighbour as yourself?

P I will, with God's help.

C Will you strive for justice and peace among all people, and respect the dignity of every human being?

P I will, with God's help.

C Let us now pray to God our Father in the words Christ gave us, and ask him for his forgiveness and protection from all evil:

Our Father . . .

The Celebrant concludes:
>Father, giver of life,
>you know how we can fail despite our resolution.
>Accept our repentant prayer
>and renew in us the grace of our baptism.
>
>We ask this through Christ our Lord.

P Amen.

Confession
Then the penitents go to the priests designated for individual confession, and confess their sins.

Final Prayer
Blessed be God the Father of our Lord Jesus Christ, who has blessed us with all the spiritual blessings of heaven in Christ.

Through water and the Holy Spirit he has delivered us from the death of sin and raised us to new life in Christ.

May we be strengthened to lead the life worthy of our vocation and preserve the unity of the Spirit by the peace that binds us together: for there is one Lord, one faith, one baptism, and one God who is Father of all, over all, through all and within all:
to him be glory and praise for ever and ever.
P Amen.

P May almighty God bless you, the Father, and the Son, and the Holy Spirit.
*All*Amen.

Recessional Hymn

LENT II

Patrick Rogers CP

This is a general-purpose penance service whose lines could be used in Lent or Advent, with some adaptation of the readings and hymns to suit the season. My focus is on the details of the ceremony, of which Guidelines should be photocopied, so as to provide a copy to each confessor and others directly involved, especially readers, organist, preacher.

It is well to have a short "briefing" of all the confessors in the sacristy, about 10 minutes before the ceremony begins, indicating how they will be positioned in the church for the confessions, and requesting them to refrain from all unnecessary questioning of the penitents, and from any but the briefest words of counsel and encouragement at that time.

The Guidelines could take a form rather like the following:

1. Sacristy
Short prayer for the confessors. A reminder of the format recommended for the individual confessions. (Refrain from unnecessary questioning, etc.).

2. Procession & Hymn
All the confessors, wearing soutane (or habit) and stole, process to sanctuary, genuflect and remain on sanctuary throughout all of the preparatory phase (i.e. up to confessions).

3. Exposition of the Blessed Sacrament
Exposition of the Blessed Sacrament is done by the Parish Priest, while the opening hymn is still being sung. Incensation. Then PP takes his seat in the Sanctuary, with the other priests.

4. Introductory Greetings and Prayer
The Co-ordinating Celebrant ("CC") uses a standard greeting ("Grace and Peace. . ."), then invites the people to sit. Briefly explains the value of "communal repentance and reconciliation". Asks them to bow their heads for the opening Prayer.

"Lord, you know me through and through. It is only in your presence that I am fully understood, both in my good points and in my sins. With you there is mercy and fullness of redemption. Give me an honest awareness of what is wrong in my life, and a generous willingness to change whatever needs to be changed. Help me to make up for any harm I have caused to others; and forgive all my offences against you, most loving Lord".

5. Liturgy of the Word

Scripture, as at Mass: First Reading, e.g. Isaiah Ch 1 (Red as scarlet/white as snow).
Responsorial (sung?) Psalm.
Gospel.
Preacher: Sermon on the welcome God has for all who turn to him.

6. Examination of Conscience

May be done, in alteration between two or more priests (eg. the Preacher and the CC) in a prayerful form.

Points for the Examination of Conscience

"Lord, you search my heart and know me through and through. . . Help me to recognise the areas in which I have sinned:

Have I. . .

(Reverence) — loved you, with all my heart and soul?
enquired about your holy will in my regard?
tried to keep your commandments?

— been unfaithful to personal prayer each day? and to Sunday Mass?
received the holy Eucharist frequently, with faith and devotion?

— honoured your blessed name?
refrained from swearing, blasphemy, indecent language? taken your name in vain?

— trusted fully in you, at all times.

(Justice) — shown kindness, respect and understanding towards my neighbour?

— given a fair day's work for fair day's pay? (and vice versa)?

— stolen or damaged goods belonging to another?

— withheld payment of my lawful debts including taxes?

— made false claims, for things I had no right to get?

— been reckless about the life and safety of other people?

— taken or distributed drugs that are injurious to health?

— threatened the livelihood of others, by unfair practices?

— driven, or been abusive, while under the influence of alcohol?

— taken the character of others, by detraction or plain slander?

— neglected to help the poor and needy, from what I could spare?

— taken care of my own family according to my state in life?

— exploited sexuality (my own or another's) outside the proper ways?

(Family) — been loyal and faithful in my family life?

— treated my partner (or fiancé) with proper respect and love?

— avoided fornication, adultery and loose behaviour? (immoral books and TV)?

— shared my income honestly and openly with the family?

— taken a proper, active interest in the children's education?

— spent time with them? let them see that I love them?

— explained right and wrong to them, according to their age?

— given them good example, by my own attitudes and actions?

— supported other people's family life, by encouragement and sympathy?

— tried to observe the kind of purity proper to my state in life?

Lord, if I have committed serious sin in any of the areas, let me have the courage to admit it honestly and repent of it from my heart. May the light of your truth shine on my mind, and the warmth of your peace be in my heart.

7. General Confession of Sins
Confiteor and Act of Contrition.

Our Father.

8. Guidelines for the Individual Confessions
The emphasis is on having the right frame of mind for receiving the mercy of God. It will be enough to say to the priest something like the following: 'Father, I am sorry for all my sins, and in particular for. . . (here you mention any serious sins you are aware of). . . and anything else in which I have offended almighty God.'

The Confessor will give you absolution. There is no need to repeat the Act of Contrition, which we have all recited together.

While the individual confessions are heard, the rest of the congregation joins in quiet meditation, with the help of prayers and hymns and silent pauses. Please remain until the end of the ceremony, which will be Benediction of the Blessed Sacrament.

Confessors at their stations around the church; preferably standing (though seated is all right if a confessor is too tired to stand). Stewards should guide the penitents, so that a short queue is formed before each priest, minimum of 12 feet clearance between penitent and queue! Priest might place his hands on the penitent's shoulders as a gesture of welcome, and in this way reassure those who are nervous and afraid.

10. Communal Prayer Penance

All the Confessors return to sanctuary where the CC leads a prayer of penance, common to all. This could be the "En Ego" or Saint Francis of Assisi's Prayer for Peace, etc.

11. Benediction and Conclusion

Parish Priest incenses, while hymn is sung. Then blesses the people (possibly processing down centre aisle, with the monstrance). Deposes Blessed Sacrament, while curate recites the Divine Praises. PP may wish to say some words of thanks to all concerned, just before the concluding hymn (*Amazing Grace* or *Let there be Peace*).

ALL SAINTS/ALL SOULS

Oliver Crilly

Entrance Song

Greeting

P In the name of the Father, and of the Son and of the Holy Spirit.

℞ Amen.

P The Lord be with you.

℞ And also with you.

Introduction

Every time we pray, we join in with the prayer of the whole Church, not just on earth, but the prayer of the whole communion of saints. They welcome us and embrace us and bring us close to God our Father.

Let us feel embraced by all our saints during this penitential service, as they help us through God's grace to come closer to one another and to God's forgiving love.

Opening Prayer

P Let us pray.
God, our Father,
we gather before you in our weakness and sinfulness,
repentent and sorrowful for our sins,
for what we have done and failed to do.
But we gather also in hope,
because we gather as your people,
united in the Church and in the Communion of Saints.
We ask you to cleanse and renew us,
and as you in your mercy forgive us,
we ask you to help us through the power of your Holy Spirit
to forgive one another.

Grant this through Christ our Lord.

℞ Amen.

LITURGY OF THE WORD

First Reading   Rom 6:2b-13

A reading from the letter of St Paul to the Romans.

Consider yourselves dead to sin but alive to God.

We are dead to sin, so how can we continue to live in it? You have been taught that when we were baptised in Christ Jesus we were baptised in his death; in other words, when we were baptised we went into the tomb with him and joined him in death, so that as Christ was raised from the dead by the Father's glory, we too might live a new life.

If in union with Christ we have imitated his death, we shall also imitate him in his resurrection. We must realise that our former selves have been crucified with him to destroy this sinful body and to free us from the slavery of sin. When a man dies, of course, he has finished with sin.

But we believe that having died with Christ we shall return to life with him: Christ, as we know, having been raised from the dead will never die again. Death has no power over him any more. When he died, he died, once for all, to sin, so his life now is life with God; and in that way, you too must consider yourselves to be dead to sin but alive for God in Christ Jesus.

That is why you must not let sin reign in your mortal bodies or command your obedience to bodily passions, why you must not let any part of your body turn into an unholy weapon fighting on the side of sin; you should, instead, offer yourselves to God, and consider yourselves dead men brought back to life; you should make every part of your body into a weapon fighting on the side of God; and then sin will no longer dominate your life, since you are living by grace and not by law.

This is the word of the Lord.

℟ Thanks be to God.

Responsorial Psalm   Ps 31:1-7

RESPONSE: Lord, forgive the wrong I have done.

1. Happy the man whose offence is forgiven,
   whose sin is remitted.
   O happy the man to whom the Lord imputes no guilt,
   in whose spirit is no guile. ℟

2. I kept it secret and my frame was wasted.
   I groaned all day long
   for night and day your hand was heavy upon me.
   Indeed, my strength was dried up as by the summer's heat. ℟

3. But now I have acknowledged my sins;
   my guilt I did not hide.
   I said: 'I will confess my offences to the Lord.'
   And you, Lord, have forgiven the guilt of my sin. ℟

4. So let every good man pray for you in the time of need.
   The floods of water may reach high
   but him they shall not reach.
   You are my hiding place, O Lord; you save me from distress.
   You surround me with cries of deliverance. ℟

Gospel Acclamation   Jn 8:12
Alleluia! Alleluia.
I am the light of the world.
Anyone who follows me
will have the light of life.
Alleluia!

Gospel   Mt 4:12-17
A reading from the holy Gospel according to Matthew.

Repent, for the kingdom of heaven is close at hand.
Hearing that John had been arrested Jesus went back to Galilee, and
leaving Nazareth he went and settled in Capernaum, a lakeside town
on the borders of Zebulun and Naphtali. In this way the prophecy
of Isaiah was to be fulfilled:

Land of Zebulun! Land of Naphtali!
Way of the sea on the far side of Jordan,
Galilee of the nations!
The people that lived in darkness has seen a great light;
on those who dwell in the land and shadow of death
a light has dawned.

From that moment Jesus began his preaching with the message,
'Repent, for the kingdom of heaven is close at hand.'

This is the Gospel of the Lord.

℟ Praise to you, Lord Jesus Christ.

Homily

If we think of saints only as those very famous people who have been canonised by the Church, we are missing something. Because we all have our own saints — all those in our own family and in our own parish who "have gone before us in the sign of faith". These are all the women and men, girls and boys, married, single, religious, priests, and even babies who have died and make up that part of the family of God who are in heaven or in purgatory.

The people of the Church on earth are sometimes called the faithful, and those who have gone before us are called the faithful departed. It's a good description; because our people who have gone before us — our own saints — have been *faithful to us*. That applies in a special way to parents and grandparents, uncles and aunts, teachers, religious and priests who have taught us and influenced us, but all our saints not only have been faithful to us, but *are* faithful to us.

It's not just that we pray for them — they pray for us and are near us in the love of God. Can you imagine our saints praying for us: "May they have rest and peace, and may the light of God's love shine on them"?

It is sin that disturbs the peace of our lives, of our minds and hearts, and it is sin that blocks out the light of God's loving presence and makes us forget about him. When we think of our faithful people praying for us, we can be sure that their greatest desire is that we should be close to God, and through being close to God that we be

39

close to them too. As we celebrate this penitential rite, let us be lifted up in the arms of all our saints into the presence of God our Father who loves us and forgives us and wants us to be fully and wholeheartedly reconciled with him and with each other. We need not be afraid, because forgiveness is only a request away.

Examination of Conscience
Some time should be given now for examination of conscience. After a period of silence, some guidelines for the examination of conscience may be given if it is considered helpful.

P The Lord is merciful. He makes us clean of heart and leads us out into his freedom when we acknowledge our guilt. Let us ask him to forgive us and bind up the wounds inflicted by our sins.

All say:
  I confess to almighty God,
  and to you, my brothers and sisters,
  that I have sinned through my own fault
  in my thoughts and in my words,
  in what I have done,
  and in what I have failed to do;
  and I ask blessed Mary, ever virgin,
  all the angels and saints,
  and you, my brothers and sisters,
  to pray for me to the Lord our God.

P Let us now pray to God our Father in the words Christ gave us, and ask him for his forgiveness and protection from all evil.

All say together:
  Our Father. . .

The priest concludes:
Lord,
through the intercession of all the saints,
help us to confess our sins
and grant us your forgiveness.
May the souls of the faithful departed rest in peace.
We ask this through Christ our Lord.

℟ Amen.

Now follows individual confession and absolution.

After the individual confessions are completed, or at an arranged time, the chief celebrant returns to the sanctuary, and addresses some words to the people, encouraging them to be thankful for the grace of repentance and forgiveness, and urging them to carry out their firm purpose of amending their lives.

The Magnificat

RESPONSE: The Lord has remembered his mercy.

1. My soul glorifies the Lord,
   my spirit rejoices in God, my Saviour.
   He looks on his servant in her lowliness;
   henceforth all ages will call me blessed. ℟

2. The Almighty works marvels for me.
   Holy is his name!
   His mercy is from age to age,
   on those who fear him. ℟

3. He puts forth his arm in strength
   and scatters the proud-hearted.
   He casts the mighty from their thrones
   and raises the lowly. ℟

4. He fills the starving with good things,
   sends the rich away empty. ℟

5. He protects Israel, his servant,
   remembering his mercy,
   the mercy promised to our fathers,
   to Abraham and his sons for ever. ℟

41

Prayer of Thanksgiving

P God our Father,
   we thank you for this experience of common prayer,
   of listening to your word,
   and especially of your love and forgiveness.
   We ask you to grant us the grace of perseverance,
   that we may serve you faithfully from now on
   in our earthly lives,
   and one day be united with all your saints
   in your heavenly kingdom.
   We ask this through Christ our Lord.
℟ Amen.

The Blessing

Then the priest blesses all present:
May the Lord guide your hearts in the way of his love
and fill you with Christ-like patience.
℟ Amen.

May he give you strength to walk in newness of life
and to please him in all things.
℟ Amen.

May almighty God bless you,
the Father, and the Son, ✠ and the Holy Spirit.
℟ Amen.

The Dismissal

The Lord has freed you from your sins. Go in peace.
℟ Thanks be to God.

PARISH CELEBRATION I
Oliver Crilly

Theme: The Beatitudes

Opening Hymn and Enthronement of the Book
During the opening hymn, the President, Readers, Homilist, Confessors and Servers process with the Lectionary and solemnly enthrone it on the lectern, where it is incensed by the President.

Greeting
P May God our Father and the Lord Jesus Christ give you grace and peace.

℞ Amen.

Opening Prayer
God our Father,
you so loved the world that you sent your only Son for our salvation.
Help us now,
as we hear again the word of that same Jesus Christ,
to acknowledge our failure to follow him
and humbly to ask your forgiveness.

We ask this through Jesus the Lord.

℞ Amen.

LITURGY OF THE WORD

A reading from the first letter of St John   1 Jn 1:5-10; 2:1-2

If we confess our sins, he is faithful and just and will forgive our sins and cleanse us from all injustice.

If we say we have no sin in us, we are deceiving ourselves and refusing to admit the truth; but if we acknowledge our sins, then God who is faithful and just will forgive our sins and purify us from everything that is wrong.

To say that we have never sinned is to call God a liar and to show that his word is not in us.

I am writing this, my children, to stop you sinning; but if anyone should sin, we have our advocate with the Father, Jesus Christ, who is just; he is the sacrifice that takes our sins away, and not only ours, but the whole world's.

This is the word of the Lord.
℞ Thanks be to God.

A brief period of silence, for personal reflection, follows the reading.

Responsorial Psalm Ps 24:4-5, 8-11, 15-18

RESPONSE: Turn to me Lord, and have mercy.

1. Lord, make me know your ways.
   Lord, teach me your paths.
   Make me walk in your truth, and teach me:
   for you are God my saviour. ℞

2. The Lord is good and upright.
   He shows the path to those who stray.
   He guides the humble in the right path;
   he teaches his way to the poor. ℞

3. His ways are faithfulness and love
   for those who keep his covenant and will.
   Lord, for the sake of your name
   forgive my guilt; for it is great. ℞

Gospel Reading
A reading from the holy Gospel according to Matthew.

Happy are the poor in spirit, for theirs is the kingdom of heaven.
Seeing the crowds, Jesus went up the hill. There he sat down and was joined by his disciples. Then he began to speak. This is what he taught them:

How happy are the poor in spirit:
theirs is the kingdom of heaven.
Happy the gentle:
they shall have the earth for their heritage.
Happy those who mourn:
they shall be comforted.
Happy those who hunger and thirst for what is right:
they shall be satisfied.
Happy the merciful:
they shall have mercy shown them.
Happy the pure in heart:
they shall see God.
Happy the peacemakers:
they shall be called sons of God.
Happy those who are persecuted in the cause of right:
theirs is the kingdom of heaven.

This is the Gospel of the Lord.

℞ Praise to you, Lord Jesus Christ.

Homily
The homily leads on to an examination of conscience and is followed by a period of silence for personal recollection.

THE SACRAMENT OF PENANCE

P My brothers and sisters, confess your sins and pray for each other,
that you may be healed.

I confess to almighty God,
and to you, my brothers and sisters,
that I have sinned through my own fault
in my thoughts and in my words,
in what I have done,
and in what I have failed to do;
and I ask blessed Mary, ever virgin,
all the angels and saints,
and you, my brothers and sisters,
to pray for me to the Lord our God.

45

P The Lord is merciful. He makes us clean of heart and leads us out into his freedom when we acknowledge our guilt. Let us ask him to forgive us and bind up the wounds inflicted by our sins.

Let us now pray to God our Father in the words Christ gave us, and ask him for his forgiveness and protection from all evil.
Our Father. . .

P Lord,
    draw near to your servants
    who in the presence of your Church
    confess that they are sinners.
    Through the ministry of the Church
    free them from all sin
    so that renewed in spirit
    they may give you thankful praise.
    We ask this through Christ our Lord.
℞ Amen.

Sign of Peace
P As brothers and sisters who reconcile themselves before their Father, let us offer each other a sign of peace.

Individual Confession
Reflective music may be played during individual confessions. Enough priests should be on hand to conclude the service in a reasonable time, but if the numbers are very large, the final prayer and blessing may be said after a fixed period, with confessions continuing afterwards for the rest of the congregation.

Final Prayer
Almighty and merciful God
we thank you for your faithful love
and your faithful forgiveness.
We ask you to help us
to show in our lives the compassion and forgiveness
which you show us.

We make this prayer through Jesus the Lord.

℞ Amen.

Final Blessing

Bow your heads and pray for God's blessing.

May almighty God keep you from all harm and bless you with every good gift.

℞ Amen.

May he set his word in your heart
and fill you with lasting joy.

℞ Amen.

May you walk in his ways
always knowing what is right and good,
until you enter your heavenly inheritance.

℞ Amen.

May almighty God bless you,
the Father, and the Son ✠ and the Holy Spirit.

℞ Amen.

PARISH CELEBRATION II

Patrick Jones

Theme: God's judging and saving word.

The book of God's word could be carried in procession and become a focus of attention. The gospel sayings used in the examination of conscience could be displayed on hangings or slides.

INTRODUCTORY RITES

Song

Expressing our worship or repentance, eg. God of Mercy and Compassion (*Veritas Hymnal* pp. 73-74) or a seasonal song, eg. O Come Emmanuel (*Veritas Hymnal* p. 51).

Greeting and Introduction

In the name of the Father, and of the Son and of the Holy Spirit. Amen.

May the grace, mercy and peace of God our Father and of Christ Jesus our Lord be with you.

Tonight we gather for a service of repentance and as we begin we place the book of Gospels in our midst. Let it dominate our gathering. Let it give us direction.

The book of Gospels or lectionary is placed on the ambo.

We will listen to God's word. We will allow ourselves to be judged by God's word. But it is also a saving word, proclaiming God's mercy for all of us.

Tonight, we have come together to accept Jesus at his word: He comes to save. We gather in common prayer — asking God to show mercy to his people — and then realising that such prayer is always answered, proclaiming our praise of God's mercy.

God's ways of mercy are without limitation. What we do tonight, celebrating the sacrament of penance, is a certain way.

We must not feel in any way pressurised to act in a strange way — rather, to remember the mercy of God — that it touches each of us — to provide the occasion to celebrate the sacrament of mercy — quietly, briefly, without fuss — as a prayer — expressing our sorrow for sin and receiving pardon and peace. Because we are engaged in common prayer — please remain until the end, so that we can thank God together.

Let us pray.

God our Father, you love us. Through our sins we have drifted away from you. Help us to respond to your loving invitation to return. Grant to us a heart renewed. Recreate in us your own Spirit. We ask this. . .

LITURGY OF THE WORD

Reading   Heb 4:12-13
The word of God, like a two-edged sword, judges us and saves us.
The word of God is alive and active, sharper than any double-edged sword. It cuts all the way through, to where soul and spirit meet, to where joints and marrow come together. It judges the desires and thoughts of man's heart.

There is nothing that can be hidden from God; everything in all creation is exposed and lies open before his eyes. And it is to him that we must all give an account of ourselves.

Psalm
eg. Grant to us, O Lord (*Alleluia! Amen!* p. 56)

Gospel   Lk 15:11-32

Is it possible to have a renewed heart? Yes. Jesus assures us that our Father in heaven will answer and welcome us.

Jesus went on to say, "There was once a man who had two sons. The younger one said to him, 'Father, give me my share of the property now.' So the man divided his property between his two sons. After a few days the younger son sold his part of the property and left home with the money. He went to a country far away, where he wasted his money in reckless living. He spent everything he had. Then a severe famine spread over that country, and he was left without a thing. So he went to work for one of the citizens of that country, who sent him out to his farm to take care of the pigs. He wished he could fill himself with the bean pods the pigs ate, but no one gave him anything to eat. At last he came to his senses and said, 'All my father's hired workers have more than they can eat, and here I am about to starve! I will get up and go to my father and say, Father, I have sinned against God and against you. I am no longer fit to be called your son; treat me as one of your hired workers.' So he got up and started back to his father.

"He was still a long way from home when his father saw him; his heart was filled with pity, and he ran, threw his arms round his son, and kissed him. 'Father,' the son said, 'I have sinned against God and against you. I am no longer fit to be called your son.' But the father called his servants. 'Hurry!' he said. 'Bring the best robe and put it on him. Put a ring on his finger and shoes on his feet. Then go and get the prize calf and kill it, and let us celebrate with a feast! For this son of mine was dead, but now he is alive; he was lost, but now he has been found.' And so the feasting began.

"In the meantime the elder son was out in the field. On his way back, when he came close to the house, he heard the music and dancing. So he called one of the servants and asked him, 'What's going on?' 'Your brother has come back home,' the servant answered, 'and your father has killed the prize calf, because he got him back safe and sound.'

"The elder brother was so angry that he would not go into the house; so his father came out and begged him to come in. But he answered his father, 'Look, all these years I have worked for you like a slave, and I have never disobeyed your orders. What have you given me? Not even a goat for me to have a feast with my friends! But this son of yours wasted all your property on prostitutes, and when he comes back home, you kill the prize calf for him!' 'My son,' the father answered, 'you are always here with me, and everything I have is yours. But we had to celebrate and be happy, because your brother was dead, but now he is alive; he was lost, but now he has been found.' "

Homily

1. We have heard the story of the Prodigal Son so often — probably the best story of the Bible.

   We know it is a parable — and that the important thing about a parable is its message or moral. And we know the moral — God is like the forgiving father. He accepts the sinner, like the father accepted the prodigal son.

2. We know all this — so much so that we run the danger of underplaying it.

   We make great claims about God because of this parable — he is, above all, a God of forgiveness — his forgiveness is without limit. God remains, always and simply, a forgiving God.

   Now let us capture the atmosphere of the story — the atmosphere of forgiveness and reconciliation. We have it here. As a people, we are sinful. It is worth acknowledging it because we know that there is a great welcome for the sinner. God is comfortable in the presence of sinners. He rushes out to meet the sinner.

   It is worth examining our consciences, our lives. The sinner has something to say. Open your heart like the son, realise your sinfulness.

   Of course, God knows it all — even better than we know ourselves. The father did not have to listen to the son's prepared speech. He wanted his son home.

The father does not give out. He does not even get as far as saying to the son that he should behave himself in the future.

And that's the moral of the story — God wants to do likewise with us.

We are faced with a God who has mercy without limit. Yes, we are talking about a limitless gift of grace. We are celebrating that gift among us.

3. Ask.

Accept.

Place your sinfulness before God. There is no older brother questioning, angry, unforgiving. There is only a forgiving Father. The focus of attention is not on us — or our sins — but on the love and mercy of God.

There is only a God who is the Father of mercies, who through the death and resurrection of his Son, Jesus, has reconciled the world to himself and sent the Holy Spirit among us for the forgiveness of our sins.

4. The only difficulty that can exist is on our part. The forgiving Father is prepared to rush out and embrace us. All we need to do is to move in his direction.

Examination of Conscience
It is best that the following is spoken by a number of people.

Let us examine our lives and assess our living in the light of the Gospel.

God's word will prompt us, jolt us, judge us and save us. We will realise the sinfulness of our lives and accept God's mercy and forgiveness.

1. Jesus said, "Repent, for the Kingdom of heaven is close at hand" (*Mt* 4:17).

   Is there serious sin in my life?
   Since my last confession, have I made a real effort to improve?
   Have I lived at peace with God? with others?

2. Jesus said "You shall love the Lord your God with all your heart, with all your soul, and with all your mind" (*Mt* 22:37).

   Do I love God with all my heart? Is there any other god — success, pleasure, wealth, possessions, self — that comes before him?
   Do I try to pray each day?
   Do I respect and reverence God's name?
   Am I faithful to Sunday Mass?

3. Jesus said "I give you a new commandment: love one another" (*Jn* 13:34).

   Have I tried to love my neighbour as myself?
   Have I helped those in need? Have I been aware of their needs?
   Have I remembered the sick, the deprived, those whom we put on the margins of our society?
   Have I been a faithful and loving member of my family?
   Have I contributed to building a happy home and family?
   Have I loved and honoured my parents?
   Have I sinned against chastity?

4. Jesus said "Happy those who hunger and thirst for what is right: they shall be satisfied" (*Mt* 5:6).

   Am I selfish, self-seeking, caring only for my own wants and needs?
   Have I respected the rights of others?
   Do I pay fair wages and provide proper working conditions?
   Do I overcharge? make false claims?
   Am I guilty of stealing? Have I stolen or damaged other people's property? Do I respect public property?
   Do I respect life? Am I conscious of other people's safety?
   Do I drive with care?
   Have I lied in a serious way?

5. Jesus said "Peace I leave with you, my own peace I give you" (*Jn* 14:27).

   Am I a person of peace?
   Do I support, condone, encourage violence in any form?
   Have I been violent, in word or action?
   Am I a source of trouble or discontent at home, at work?

6. Jesus said "You are the salt of the earth. . ., the light of the world" (*Mt* 5:13-14).

   Am I willing to be counted as a Christian?

7. Jesus said "Courage, your sins are forgiven" (*Mt* 9:2).

LITURGY OF RECONCILIATION

General Confession of Sins

Lord Jesus, you forgive us our sins. Lord, have mercy.

Lord Jesus, you bring peace to our world. Lord, have mercy.

Lord Jesus, you embrace us in friendship. Lord, have mercy.

Lord Jesus, you promise us life. Lord, have mercy.

Lord Jesus, you welcome us home. Lord, have mercy.

Lord Jesus, you give us the promise of everlasting life.
                                        Lord, have mercy.

I confess to almighty God. . .

Our Father. . .

O my God I thank you for loving me.
I am sorry for all my sins,
for not loving others and not loving you.
Help me to live like Jesus and not sin again.

A familiar Act of Sorrow may be added.

Individual Confession and Absolution

We have the opportunty to celebrate the sacrament of penance. Approach any of the priests — be free to move around the church, to any of the priests. Allow people privacy by staying back a little.

Say something like "I am sorry for all my sins and I want forgiveness". Mention serious sins as best you can. In other words, make a simple, a brief, a sincere confession of sin. You don't have to say any more. We already have expressed our sorrow.

The priest will pray the prayer of absolution. Return to your place — pray for one another.

The Rite of Penance provides a primary source for suitable hymns, psalms and prayers that may be used during this period of the service.

Proclamation of praise of God's mercy
Let us proclaim God's mercy and give him thanks.
Magnificat (*Alleluia! Amen!* p. 122).

Concluding prayer of thanksgiving
Let us pray

God our Father, through the greatness of your love
we have access to your house.
You have renewed the love we have wasted.
We praise you. We thank you.
We make our prayer through Christ our Lord.
Amen.

Final Blessing
We have proclaimed and celebrated God's promise of forgiveness.

May the Father lavish his love upon you. Amen.

May Christ support you. Amen.

May the Spirit fill you with joy. Amen.

May almighty God, the Father and the Son and the Holy Spirit, bless you. Amen.

Offer each other the sign of peace.

Go in that peace.

PARISH CELEBRATION III

Johnny Doherty CSSR

The lighting in the Church should be subdued with a spotlight on a Cross or Crucifix.

Opening Hymn

During the opening hymn, the Book of the Scriptures is carried in in solemn procession, which should include all those who are to hear confessions; the book is solemnly enthroned near the Crucifix and it is then incensed, after which the congregation is also incensed.

P   We are gathered together to celebrate the wonder of our salvation. In the Cross we have a powerful sign that our salvation has already taken place. In the Sacrament of Reconciliation we have the sign that our salvation is yet to be made complete in us. We are sinners, constantly in need of forgiveness.

That is one of the great paradoxes of our faith: we are saved, and yet to be saved. The Sacrament of Reconciliation is part of the saving power that Christ has given his Church.

A good model for us to bring with us this evening is St Dismas:

a) He was a thief.

b) He was very close to Jesus as our Saviour died on the Cross.

c) He made one of the most amazing acts of faith, when he said: "Lord, remember me when you come into your kingdom." Jesus looked like anything but the Son of God at that moment.

d) He teaches us that forgiveness is immediate and complete. "This day you will be with me in paradise," Jesus said.

Prayer

Lord Jesus Christ,
we thank you for showing us how much you love us
by dying on a Cross that we might live.
Strengthen us.

We pray that each of us here may have true repentance for our sins and ask forgiveness and healing in this Sacrament which you gave your Church.

We pray that each one may be filled with hope in your love rather than despair because of the bonds of sin in our lives.

Take away all anxiety and fear from our hearts, and, as our sins are forgiven again this evening, strengthen us to live in ways that will make it easier for others to know your love and to live your way.

Lord Jesus Christ, we pray to you as our Saviour.

We know you as Son of God, who lives and reigns with the Father and the Holy Spirit, God for ever and ever.

℞ Amen.

Hymn

Gospel   Mt 18:1-4
A reading from the holy Gospel according to Matthew.

At that time the disciples came to Jesus, asking, "Who is the greatest in the kingdom of heaven?"

So Jesus called a child, made him stand in front of them, and said, "I assure you that unless you change and become like children, you will never enter the Kingdom of heaven. The greatest in the Kingdom of heaven is the one who humbles himself and becomes like this child."

This is the Gospel of the Lord.

℞ Praise to you, Lord Jesus Christ.

Homily and Examination of Conscience
We may not want to be "the greatest" in heaven, but we do want to get there. Jesus tells us that, to get there, we must become like little children.

Children have many qualities that are essential for living as God's children:

Trust: Look at a child in the arms of its parents; are we like that in our relationship with God?

Enthusiasm: Children look forward to almost everything; we take almost everything for granted.

Wonder: Look at a child at Christmas; the box is as important as the toy. We pass our days surrounded by beauty and we don't even notice it.

Forgiveness: A child can have a fight with someone one moment, and the next, be friends. We hold grudges until the other person has been punished.

Innocence: Children ask a lot of questions and say a lot of outrageous things, but we can smile at them because we recognise the basic innocence of their minds and hearts. We have learned to be cautious, to manipulate, to be devious in so many ways. Often we have learned this as the way to survive.

When we examine our lives with the eyes of a child, we can easily find the ways in which we have to repent of our sins and to change so as to regain the freedom that God's grace brings us. We will go back over those same headings and apply them more fully to ourselves:

Trust: We live in a world which is increasingly becoming materialistic. You have to look after number one. There is no room for trust in God's way of justice if you are going to get on in the world. That is so readily accepted today that it is destroying us.

— Do I do an honest day's work for an honest day's pay?

— Do I pay an honest wage to those who work for me? Or do I pay the minimum?

— Do I falsify tax returns and so put a burden on others?

— Do I take my place in fighting injustice in our society or do I leave it to others and so contribute to that injustice?

— Do I contribute to supporting the poor or do I see that what's mine is my own and has no reference to anyone else?

Innocence: When we say that someone has lost their innocence, we usually mean it in sexual terms. That is much too narrow an application because it involves our whole way of life. Our sexuality is central to life and how we use our sexuality is significant in our response to God's desire for us.

— In reading books, papers, magazines, do I often look for sexual excitement?
— What do I look for in the TV programmes I watch or the films I go to?
— How do I regard my own body? Do I abuse my gift of sexuality by masturbation?
— In my relationships with others do I follow God's way or is my standard simply: "If I feel like it, I do it."?
— Do I try to reverence the sexual dignity of others? Do I fail in this?
— Do I live by the standard of God's law that sexual intercourse is for marriage?
— In marriage, do I *use* my spouse sexually? Is there a lot of affection in how I treat her/him, or is intercourse simply an activity?
— Do I use sex in marriage as a bargaining power or as the free gift of myself?

Enthusiasm: Lift a child in the air and, when you put him/her down again, you'll almost always be asked: "Do it again!" And if there's another child there, you'll be asked: "Do it to me too!"

— Is that the way I am with God and the things of God?
— Do I pray every day? Or does it depend on how I feel?
— Is my prayer enthusiastic or a bit of a drag?
— Do I go to Mass every Sunday and Holyday?
— Do I take an active part in the Mass or do I leave it to others to get on with it?
— Do I even consider the possibility of going to Mass during the week?
— Do I go to confession regularly?

— Am I open and honest when I go to confession?
— Am I involved in the parish in any active way?
— Am I willing to be involved in new ways to build up the life of the parish?

Sense of wonder: In adults, we see the loss of a sense of wonder about life. Drink, and in more recent times, drugs are such signs. These are entered into and abused most often out of boredom or a search for some "kick" out of life. They only lead to a further diminishing of the spirit.

— Do I drink to excess?
— How does my drinking affect my family and my friends?
— Do I encourage others to drink more than they want?
— Do I take drugs?
— Do I encourage others to take drugs?
— Do I spend a lot of money on my own pleasure and entertainment?
— Do I gamble a lot on horses, dogs etc.?

Forgiveness: Children don't hold grudges for very long. Adults can hold grudges for a lifetime.

— Is there anyone whom I find difficult to forgive?
— Who or what makes me angry in my family life, my life in Church, my work life, my social life?
— Do I talk about and criticise particular people?
— Whom have I hurt by an angry word or action in my family, among my friends?
— Is there anyone in my family on whom I have given up and only meet when I have to?

We now publicly admit that each of us is a sinner. Let us say together:
I confess. . .

We also publicly acknowledge our sorrow by saying together an Act of Contrition.

Let us pray together in the words our Saviour gave us;
Our Father . . .

Address before Confession
The priests will now go to various parts of the church. They will stand and you will stand with them. Ask him for either a blessing or for absolution. You may not need confession tonight — maybe because you were at this Sacrament very recently or perhaps you may not be able to receive the Sacrament at the moment because of something in your life. Mention that to the priest and he will pray with you and bless you in the name of the Church.

If you want absolution, say that to the priest and then simply tell him the sins that you are conscious of.

The priest will place his hands on your shoulders to express the affection the Church has for each one of us and also to make it easier to speak without being heard by others.

This is not a time for getting into discussion with the priest or seeking advice about a particular problem. Leave that, please, for another time.

When you have told your sins, the priest will give you absolution.

No need to say the Act of Contrition as we have said it together already.

During this time we will pray and sing together. We will say the rosary and sing a hymn between each decade. In this way we can pray for one another right through this sacred time.

When everyone has had a chance to speak to a priest, we will all gather again for a final prayer and blessing.

Notes: Have the Rosary arranged beforehand, with people deputed to lead it, special intentions for each decade which reflect the repentance and reconciliation of the parish and with hymns for between each decade.

The priests should begin the process of individual confession by asking each other for a blessing or absolution just as we are asking our people to do.

Final Prayer and Blessing

After the individual confessions, the priests should all go to the front of the sanctuary, face the people and, as the leader prays, all the priests extend their hands over the congregation.

P May God, the Father of mercies,
   through the intercession of our Blessed Lady
   fill your hearts and your homes with his peace.
   May he take away from you all anxiety and fear.
   May he heal all divisions that exist in your families
   and in our parish community
   and may he bless all those you love.
   Together with them, may he bring you to everlasting life.

℟ Amen.

P May almighty God bless you,
   the Father, and the Son, ✠ and the Holy Spirit.

℟ Amen.

Final Hymn "City of God"

SMALL GROUP I
Pierce Murphy

Theme: Pure Religion

Opening Hymn
eg. "Grant to us O Lord, a heart renewed"
or the psalm with refrain.

Introduction
We have been together for some time now struggling to increase our
faith, to broaden our hope and deepen our love of God and of our
neighbour. We come to look at our lives in relation to God our Father,
to see our strengths and our weaknesses; to confess to our loving and
forgiving God and to be joyfully reconciled with him and with each
other. Then we can live as true sons and daughters of our God.

We have chosen the theme of "Pure Religion" or, put it another
way, — "what does God ask of me, of us?" Our reflection comes
from the Prophet Micah. He has been reminding the people of the
great wonders Yahweh, their God, has done for them. They want
to respond. They want to respond with sacrifices and burnt offerings.
Then Micah gives Yahweh's answer as follows:

Reader:
This is what God asks of you,
only this: to act justly,
          love tenderly
          and to walk humbly with your God. (*Micah 6:8*)

This is the word of the Lord.

℟ Amen.

*Reader or celebrant leads the reflection. The group could be invited to share
on some or all of the points:*
Does this passage surprise you?
Does it remind you of anything Jesus said? (Mt 25 "Did it to me")

63

Let us take each sentence:

To act justly

Reflection: We can see people doing their everyday jobs with care, concern and honesty. They know that they are lucky to have jobs and are concerned for others. Many a mother, or indeed a father now, spends their time quietly rearing a family to take their place in society and have good Christian values. An eagerness to work with a sense of fair play or justice are some of the values they pass on. They are very generous to people in need, both those near at home and those in the third world countries. Many young people are really incensed at the exploitation, poverty and destruction, often caused by greed for possessions or for power. They actively work to relieve this. Sometimes we see people who seem to have a double standard of justice when they are dealing with the Government or big business. Other times people, by their unfair comments or gossip, can ruin another person or company.

Points to ponder:
Am I lazy or energetic?
Do I think of others or am I selfish?
How am I concerned for people who are starving?
Are my comments about others fair and just?
What is my attitude in dealing with the Government, pensions etc?
How do I treat my employer and his property and time?

Sharing if appropriate
Period of Silence (Music)

Prayer
Priest: God our Father be with us as we struggle to act justly in our lives. Help us to realise that we have a lot. Help us to have a spirit of openess and generosity in our lives so that we can show your love to others. This we ask through Christ our Lord. Amen.

Love Tenderly

Reflection: The values which produce tender love between people don't come from television or novels, they come from deep within us. They reflect the fact that God loved us first and has made us for his love. Whether we are married or single these values enable us to be life-giving for others. Often these values are not there in some of our relationships and there is often a gruff selfishness that sees others as objects, objects to be used or to give pleasure.

We can contrast this with the homely picture of a father or mother picking up the child for the nth time at night, or the husband and wife settling near the fire to relax and talk together when the family are in bed, or the wife in the kitchen preparing the family meals and seeing her worth before God, or the husband who works hard for his family and takes only one drink in the pub so that he can spend more time with his family; or the young couple in love, tenderly yet respectfully preparing for their marriage, or the teenage family who respectfully and lovingly work to make their home happy.

Points to ponder:
How can I love my partner more tenderly?
How can I spend more time with him/her?
Do I see people as people to be loved or used?
How can I help people grow in love rather than
    stunt their growth?
What people do I exclude from my love?
Am I faithful to my partner, to my friends?
Do I pass on God's pattern for loving or the media's?

Sharing if appropriate

Period of Silence (Music)

Prayer

Priest: God our Father, it is your love of us that inspires our love of others. Help our love to grow more tender so that your love in us will reach perfection. This we ask through Christ our Lord. Amen.

Walk humbly with God

Reflection: Jesus told the story of the Pharisee and the tax-collector. The tax-collector clearly saw his position before God and would only stand at the door asking for forgiveness. He knew his strengths and weaknesses before God. We know that we are made in the image and likeness of our God and that gives us a great dignity and worth. We also know that without God's help we have little or no chance of living up to that dignity. If we leave God out of our lives we are putting ourselves at the centre of our world and very often we leave ourselves there in our frustration with ourselves. With God all things are possible. So in our daily prayer we can praise God for his great love of us, ask his help for the future and beg his pardon for the past.

Points to ponder:
Where does God come into my life?
How can I give more time to prayer?
Do I praise and thank God, especially at Mass?
Do I thank God for my successes or just blame him
    for my failures?
How do I respect God and his name?
Do I respect others who walk with God too?

Sharing if appropriate

Period of Silence (Music)

Psalm 51

RESPONSE: Have mercy on me, God in your kindness,
            in your compassion blot out my offence.

A pure heart create for me, O God,
put a steadfast spirit within me.
Do not cast me from your presence
nor deprive me of your holy spirit. ℟

O rescue me, God, my helper
and my tongue shall ring out your goodness.
O Lord, open my lips
and my mouth shall declare your praise. ℟

For in sacrifice you take no delight,
burnt offering from me you would refuse,
my sacrifice, a contrite spirit.
A humbled, contrite heart you will not spurn. ℞

Reading
Micah again or James 1:19-27 *or Mt* 25:31-36

Act of Sorrow
For the injustices I have caused to others, directly or indirectly.
Lord, have mercy. ℞

For the lack of love in my life especially for those close to me.
Christ, have mercy. ℞

For the times I have made myself the centre of my life.
Lord, have mercy. ℞

All

I confess. . .
P Let us pray together in the words our Saviour gave us:
All Our Father . . .

If there is to be sacramental confession, the individual confessions now take place. Alternatively, the Service may simply be concluded with a prayer for forgiveness like:

May almighty God have mercy on us,
forgive us our sins
and bring us to life everlasting. Amen.
(*from the Penitential Rite of Mass*)

Celebrant:
Let us give each other a sign of peace —
a sign of the surety of God's forgiveness
and an offer of support for the future. . .

Psalm of Thanks
eg Ps 136 v 1, 2, 3, 4, 6, 23, 24, 25, 26.
Response: For his love endures forever.

Priest leads prayer together:
God, Father of the humble walkers,
be with us in each new step,
guide our faltering feet,
warm our cool hearts,
sustain our just dealings
as we struggle to make your world a better place to live in.

This we ask through Christ our Lord.

℞ Amen.

Priest:
Go in peace to walk with God.

℞ Amen.

Hymn
eg 'Hymn of Micah' or 'Christ be with me'.

SMALL GROUP II
New Year's Eve: Family Celebration

I used this simple adaptation of Young People II (James Doherty) for a very successful family celebration at midnight on New Year's Eve.
— *Oliver Crilly*

I: PENITENTIAL RITE

Taize music

Crucifix in centre. Candle lighted before it. Two groups of children enter from opposite sides, in dark clothes, and glare at each other. Hold position. Then slowly they all turn to face the crucifix. They turn slowly to look at each other again, take off their jackets or coats to reveal white shirts or tops or brightly coloured dresses. They step towards each other, take each other's hands, and make peace. Then they all simply kneel before the crucifix. They stay kneeling for the reading.

Gospel Mt 5:23-24

A reading from the holy Gospel according to Matthew.

If you are about to offer your gift to God at the altar, and there you remember that your brother has something against you, leave your gift there in front of the altar, go at once and make peace with your brother, and then come back and offer your gift to God.

This is the Gospel of the Lord.

℞ Praise to you, Lord Jesus Christ.

Intercessions

For the times when we have allowed our feelings to rule our lives and make us hurtful to those around us, Lord, have mercy.

℞ Lord, have mercy.

For the times we have closed our fists and our hearts to others, Lord, have mercy. ℞

For the times we have refused to walk with our brothers and sisters, Lord, have mercy. ℟

Let us pray together in the words Jesus gave us:
Our Father. . .

Taize music

Each person present goes forward in his or her turn, kneels for quite a long time in front of the crucifix, asking God's forgiveness and offering their life to God to try to do his will in the New Year. Then they return quietly to their place. All say together the Act of Sorrow.

II: HYMNS AND READINGS
A Liturgy of the Word follows, to the following outline:

Hymn
First Reading
Psalm
Second Reading
Alleluia verse
Gospel
Short shared reflection

Taize music

Each person receives a picture of Christ, the ruler of all the world. A candle is lighted and brought in procession to the table where everyone will have some food and drink, the first shared meal of the New Year.

YOUNG PEOPLE I

Joe McDermott

Opening Hymn   PP92 -   *Here I Am Lord*
Father Mercy

(Songs of the Saint Louis Jesuits Comprehensive Ed. © 1977, 1978, North American Liturgy Resources.)

Celebrant: In the Name of the Father and of the Son and of the Holy Spirit
All: Amen.

C: The peace of the Lord be with you always.
All: And also with you.

C: In our lives we experience, on the one hand, goodness, peace, joy and love — and on the other, evil, pain, suffering and hatred. These are caused by people. Within each of us is the potential for good and for evil. It is difficult, even painful, to confront ourselves with the reality of our own lives, and to take responsibility for the pain and suffering we have caused to others. God calls us to grow. We want to change, and we know we can. Through Jesus we are assured of God's love and forgiveness.

The pain and suffering that Jean Vanier noticed in his book, *Be Not Afraid* is the same pain and suffering that touches all our lives and the lives of those around us.
Let us reflect on the following passage:

If I truly love
if I feel concerned
my life must change

My life must change
the life I have built for myself

must be destroyed
must be completely changed

the time I get up and go to bed
the friends I like to talk with
               go out with
                   eat with in smart restaurants

the books I read
the money I have to spend

If I enter the world of touch
        the world of tender compassion
        the world of the prisoner, the handicapped, the hungry
my whole way of life is in danger of falling apart.
I am in danger of entering a world of insecurity.

And yet we need security
those landmarks
which let us know where we are
and perhaps let us know ourselves a little

If I become truly open
                open to the sufferings of others
my life will change
I will change
It's too much
I'm afraid.

So better cross the street
        not stop by the half-dead man
        not look at him
        not visit the prisons, the handicapped, the sick.

Or if I do stop
invent reasons
        not to become involved
        not to give myself
        not to touch them
        not to become committed.

Exciting theories!
Society had better change!
Abolish poverty!
I'll start a revolution
I'll solve everything
There won't be any more poor people!

Or I'll go back to my books
> *to my humane or revolutionary talk*
> *I'll escape to drugs, to television, to eroticism*
>> *or throw myself into hyperactivity*
>> *work to make money*
>> *not knowing how to spend*
>> *on increasingly*
>>> *useless*
>>> *suicidal luxuries*
>> *which kill*
>> *by comfort*
> *I'll escape the poor, the suffering, the forsaken*
> *I'll flee the world of compassion.*

Gospel Reading   Deacon Leon Zalewski   Lk 15:11-32
A reading from the holy Gospel according to Luke

Jesus went on to say, "There was once a man who had two sons. The younger one said to him, 'Father, give me my share of the property now.' So the man divided his property between his two sons. After a few days the younger son sold his part of the property and left home with the money. He went to a country far away, where he wasted his money in reckless living. He spent everything he had. Then a severe famine spread over that country, and he was left without a thing. So he went to work for one of the citizens of that country, who sent him out to his farm to take care of the pigs. He wished he could fill himself with the bean pods the pigs ate, but no one gave him anything to eat. At last he came to his senses and said, 'All my father's hired workers have more than they can eat, and here I am about to starve! I will get up and go to my father and say, Father, I have sinned against God and against you. I am no longer fit to be called your son; treat me as one of your hired workers.' So he got up and started back to his father.

"He was still a long way from home when his father saw him; his heart was filled with pity, and he ran, threw his arms round his son, and kissed him. 'Father,' the son said, 'I have sinned against God and against you. I am no longer fit to be called your son.' But the father called his servants. 'Hurry!' he said. 'Bring the best robe and put it on him. Put a ring on his finger and shoes on his feet. Then go and get the prize calf and kill it, and let us celebrate with a feast! For this son of mine was dead, but now he is alive; he was lost, but now he has been found.' And so the feasting began.

"In the meantime the elder son was out in the field. On his way back, when he came close to the house, he heard the music and dancing. So he called one of the servants and asked him, 'What's going on?' 'Your brother has come back home,' the servant answered, 'and your father has killed the prize calf, because he got him back safe and sound.'

"The elder brother was so angry that he would not go into the house; so his father came out and begged him to come in. But he answered his father, 'Look, all these years I have worked for you like a slave, and I have never disobeyed your orders. What have you given me? Not even a goat for me to have a feast with my friends! But this son of yours wasted all your property on prostitutes, and when he comes back home, you kill the prize calf for him!' 'My son,' the father answered, 'you are always here with me, and everything I have is yours. But we had to celebrate and be happy, because your brother was dead, but now he is alive; he was lost, but now he has been found.' "

This is the Gospel of the Lord.

℞   Praise to you, Lord Jesus Christ.

Homily
The celebrant might like to point out the stages of the reconciliation process between the Prodigal Son and his Father. The Son first came to an awareness of what he had done. He decided to do something about it. Having made his decision to change, he returned to the

Father. In the Father he encountered not the blame he had expected, but complete forgiveness. He was welcomed back as a son, not as a hired servant as he had expected.

Examination of Conscience

C: Let us reflect on our lives, so that we too may come to an awareness of our sinfulness. Let us think of the way we live with, and relate to, others.

Have I been responsible for divisions, anguish, rejection in my family? (*pause.*)

In my relationships with others, have I used people selfishly — friends, work associates, etc.? (*pause.*)

Have I been honest in my relationships and in my responsibilities? (*pause.*)

Have I offered my time, my talents, my resources to help those most in need — the poor, the marginalised, the lonely, the suffering? (*pause.*)

Have I taken responsibility for my own growth in faith? (*pause.*)

Do I make time for God through reflection, searching, prayer? (*pause.*)

Do I allow my belief in God and his message to challenge the attitudes and values which rule my life? (*pause.*)

Is my belief in God a mere habit or convention? (*pause.*)

Have I taken responsibility for building the Kingdom of God in our world — or have I opted for a kingdom based on the attitudes and values of today's world? (*pause.*)

Act of Repentance

C: Let us confess our sinfulness to God and to each other and let us ask for God's mercy and forgiveness.

All: I confess to almighty God,
and to you my brothers and sisters,
that I have sinned through my own fault,
in my thoughts, and in my words,
in what I have done
and in what I have failed to do.
And I ask Blessed Mary, ever virgin,
all the angels and saints
and you my brothers and sisters to pray for me,
to the Lord our God.

Sing   *Peace Prayer of St Francis*
either: Kyrie Eleison
or: Domine Deus, Filius Patris, Miserere nobis.
(*Taize Chants*)

Act of Sorrow

O, my God, I am heartly sorry
For all my sins, because I have offended thee,
Who art infinitely good.
And I firmly resolve with the help of thy grace,
Never to offend thee again.

C: May almighty God have mercy on us,
may he forgive us our sinfulness,
and may he bring us to the eternal Kingdom
of peace, love and joy with him forever.
All: Amen.

C: Let us pray together to the Father, in the words
Jesus taught us to use.
All: Our Father. . .

C: Deliver us Lord from every evil,
and grant us peace in our day.
In your mercy, keep us free from sin,
and protect us from all anxiety
as we wait in joyful hope
for the coming of our Saviour Jesus Christ.

All: For the kingdom, the power
and the glory are yours,
now and forever, Amen.

   C: Lord Jesus Christ,
you said to your apostles,
I leave you peace, my peace I give you.
Look not on our sins,
but on the faith of your church
and grant us the peace and unity of your kingdom
where you live forever and ever.

All: Amen.

   C: Let us now offer each other a sign of peace.

   C: Let us thank God who shows us his mercy and love
through Jesus in the story of the Prodigal Son.
Be with us Lord as we go from here. Journey with
us as we work to make your Kingdom come in our
own lives and in our world, through Christ Our
Lord.

All: Amen.

Blessing

   C: The Lord be with you.

All: And also with you.

   C: May the God of Peace
fill your hearts with every blessing.
May he sustain you
with his gifts of hope and consolation.
May he help you to offer your lives in his service
and bring you safely to eternal glory.

May almighty God, the Father, the Son, and the
Holy Spirit grant you all that is good.

All: Amen.

All confirmants & Sponsors
will go to confession

YOUNG PEOPLE II

James Doherty

Theme: Eucharist

Begin with some quiet music or a hymn.

A large crucifix is placed in the sanctuary. Two groups of two or three people each enter from opposite ends, dressed in dark clothes with dark jackets or pullovers. When they come face to face with each other, they take fixed positions and glare at each other. This position is held for a few minutes. Slowly they turn their heads until all their eyes are fixed on the crucifix. They hold this position.
Then they slowly turn and look at each other again, take off their jackets or tops to reveal white shirts or tops. They step towards each other, exchange greetings and then simply kneel before the crucifix.

As they kneel, the reading is proclaimed:

A reading from the holy Gospel according to Matthew
Mt 5:23-24

If you are about to offer your gift to God at the altar, and there you remember that your brother has something against you, leave your gift there in front of the altar, go at once and make peace with your brother, and then come back and offer your gift to God.

This is the Gospel of the Lord.

℟ Praise to you, Lord Jesus Christ.

Intercessions

For the times we have allowed our prejudices to dictate our actions,
  Lord have mercy.
℟ Lord have mercy.

For the times we have closed our fists and our hearts to others,
  Lord have mercy. ℟

For the times we have refused to walk with our brothers and sisters,
  Lord have mercy. ℟

Let us pray:

God our Father, enlighten our hearts and our minds with the light
  of your Holy Spirit.

Keep us open to others journeying with us.

Help us to be young enough to jump over the barriers of fear,
  prejudice and hatred,

that our lives may continually witness

to the life and love of Jesus Christ,

your Son, who lives and reigns with you,

in the unity of the Holy Spirit,

one God for ever and ever.

℞ Amen.

YOUNG PEOPLE III

James Doherty

Theme: Love your neighbour.

Begin with a simple hymn; a Taizé chant is quite helpful.

Then a mime follows, involving four characters. One stands on a raised platform with arms outstretched to represent God the Father. Two stand a little away, deeply engrossed in conversation. A fourth enters carrying a weight on the shoulders (a simple log or piece of wood).

The person with the burden moves slowly towards the two who are conversing; they do not even notice. Then he/she moves towards the "God person", pauses and looks up. The God person comes down to ground level, moves to the two persons talking, touches their shoulders and points to the burdened person. They move slowly towards this person, remove the burden and then all three walk side by side.

A reading from the letter of James   Jas 2:1-9

My brothers, as believers in Our Lord Jesus Christ, the Lord of Glory, you must never treat people in different ways according to their outward appearance. Supposing a rich man wearing a gold ring and fine clothes comes to your meeting, and a poor man in ragged clothes also comes. If you show more respect to the well-dressed man and say, "Have this best seat here," but say to the poor man, "Stand over there, or sit on the floor by my feet," then you are guilty of creating distinctions among yourselves and of making judgements based on evil motives.

Listen, my dear brothers! God chose the poor of this world to be rich in faith and to possess the kingdom which he promised to those who love him. But you dishonour the poor! Who are the ones who oppress you and drag you before the judges? The rich! They are the ones who speak evil of that good name which has been given to you.

You will be doing the right thing if you obey the law of the Kingdom, which is found in the scripture, "Love your neighbour as you love yourself." But if you treat people according to their outward appearance, you are guilty of sin, and the Law condemns you as a lawbreaker.

This is the word of the Lord.
℟ Thanks be to God.

Intercessions
For the times we have closed our hearts to those in need, Lord have mercy. ℟ Lord have mercy.

For the times that we have been so concerned about our own affairs that we have forgotten others, Lord have mercy. ℟

For the times that our own comfort has blinded us to the discomfort of others, Lord have mercy. ℟

Let us pray:
God our Father,
teach us to be sensitive to the living of others,
help us to show them the respect that is their due,
move us to respond to the needs of others,
that we may learn to love you and our neighbour
with one and the same love.

We make this prayer through Christ our Lord.

℟ Amen.

CHILDREN I (10-12 years old)

Maura Hyland

Introduction

Opening Hymn: Song of Hosea (Glory and Praise Vol. 3)

C: The peace of Christ be with you all.
All: And also with you.

C: We have heard God's call to us to build a Kingdom of peace, love, truth and justice. Through his son Jesus, God has shown us how to do this. We know that there are many ways in which we can build a better world at home, at school and when we are with our friends. Sometimes we work very hard to do this. Sometimes, however we are selfish and think only of ourselves and of our own needs. When we stop and think about this we realise that we must change. Jesus tells us that God is always waiting for us, always ready to forgive us. There is always time to begin again.

Liturgy of the Word

Child: I Feel Ashamed (Psalm 130)

Today dear God, I come
Needing your forgiveness.
I do not feel good about myself
When I forget your laws.

But I remember your promise of mercy.
I wait for it just as I wait for a night storm to be over,
And daylight to come.
I know you will forgive me and not remember my sins.

C: Let us listen to a story from the gospel in which Jesus shows us the forgiveness and love of God.

Gospel Reading   Lk 15:11-32

A reading from the holy Gospel according to Luke

Jesus went on to say, "There was once a man who had two sons.

82

The younger one said to him, 'Father, give me my share of the property now.' So the man divided his property between his two sons. After a few days the younger son sold his part of the property and left home with the money. He went to a country far away, where he wasted his money in reckless living. He spent everything he had. Then a severe famine spread over that country, and he was left without a thing. So he went to work for one of the citizens of that country, who sent him out to his farm to take care of the pigs. He wished he could fill himself with the bean pods the pigs ate, but no one gave him anything to eat. At last he came to his senses and said, 'All my father's hired workers have more than they can eat, and here I am about to starve! I will get up and go to my father and say, Father, I have sinned against God and against you. I am no longer fit to be called your son; treat me as one of your hired workers.' So he got up and started back to his father.

"He was still a long way from home when his father saw him; his heart was filled with pity, and he ran, threw his arms round his son, and kissed him. 'Father,' the son said, 'I have sinned against God and against you. I am no longer fit to be called your son.' But the father called his servants. 'Hurry!' he said. 'Bring the best robe and put it on him. Put a ring on his finger and shoes on his feet. Then go and get the prize calf and kill it, and let us celebrate with a feast! For this son of mine was dead, but now he is alive; he was lost, but now he has been found.' And so the feasting began.

"In the meantime the elder son was out in the field. On his way back, when he came close to the house, he heard the music and dancing. So he called one of the servants and asked him, 'What's going on?' 'Your brother has come back home,' the servant answered, 'and your father has killed the prize calf, because he got him back safe and sound.'

"The elder brother was so angry that he would not go into the house; so his father came out and begged him to come in. But he answered his father, 'Look, all these years I have worked for you like a slave, and I have never disobeyed your orders. What have you given me? Not even a goat for me to have a feast with my friends! But this son of yours wasted all your property on prostitutes, and when he comes back home, you kill the prize calf for him!' 'My son,' the father answered, 'you are always here with me, and everything I have is yours. But we had to celebrate and be happy, because your brother was dead, but now he is alive; he was lost, but now he has been found.' "

This is the Gospel of the Lord.

℞ Praise to you, Lord Jesus Christ.

Homily
The celebrant might like to help the children to reflect on the following aspects of the story.

The Prodigal Son didn't appreciate all the good things he had in his father's house. It is very easy to take for granted the love and care and comfort that we find at home.

At first the prodigal son enjoyed himself with his new friends. Sometimes we enjoy what we're doing even if it is wrong.

He was very much ashamed when he became aware of what he had done, how ungrateful he was to his father, how selfishly he had acted. Sometimes we are ashamed of what we do too. He must have found it very difficult to go back and say sorry. We too find it difficult to admit that we have been wrong.

The father did not condemn him or punish him as we would expect. He didn't make him a servant. He welcomed him back as a son. We find it difficult to understand the forgiveness of God. We find it difficult to believe that he really is ready to welcome us back no matter how bad we have been, no matter what wrongs we have done.

The older son was very jealous when he saw the fuss that was being made of his younger brother. Sometimes we too are jealous of others, of their success, or when people praise them.

Examination of Conscience
C: Let us take some time to think about our own lives and to ask ourselves if we have failed to answer God's call to build his Kingdom in our world.

Have we refused to build a better world at home:

Have we been selfish; have we refused to help out when we could; have we been conscious of the needs of others especially those older or younger than ourselves; have we been the cause of rows and arguments; have we made up again after rows or have we held grudges; when we were wrong have we admitted that we were and said sorry?
(*Pause*)

Have we refused to build a better world at school:

Have we co-operated with the teacher and with others in class when doing project work; have we refused to do our share of the tidying and cleaning in the classroom; have we done things which damage or destroy school property; have we been careless when using other peoples' books or pens or markers; have we taken other people's property and not returned it; have we refused to allow some children to join in games; have we ignored people who need our help; have we been disruptive in class?
(*Pause*)

Have we refused to build a better world in our neighbourhood:

Have we been careless about throwing litter or damaging public property; have we refused to make an effort to help people who needed help by doing messages, or by visiting old people; have we been careless on the road or done anything that would cause danger to ourselves or to others.
(*Pause*)

Have we refused to build a better world when we are playing with our friends:

Have we played fairly; have we caused rows and disagreements; have we done things to hurt others because of jealousy; have we told lies to our friends?
(*Pause*)

Have we remembered to say our prayers; have we been careless in Church; have we tried to distract others during prayer time; have we used God's name or Jesus's name with disrespect? (*Pause*)

Act of Repentance
Hymn: Grant to us O Lord a heart renewed.

C: Let us confess to God that we have not always worked to build a better world, a world of love, truth, justice and peace.

All: I confess. . .

Child: For all the times when we have been selfish and by thinking only of ourselves have caused suffering to others.
Lord have mercy.

All: Lord have mercy.

Child: For all the times when we have caused rows and arguments, when we have refused to say sorry, when we have not admitted that we were wrong when we told lies and were dishonest.
Christ have mercy.

All: Christ have mercy.

Child: For all the times when we didn't bother to say our prayers, when we didn't pay attention at Mass, when we disturbed others, when we used God's name in disrespect.
Lord have mercy.

All: Lord have mercy.

C: Let us pray together the act of sorrow.

All: O my God, I thank you for loving me. . .

C.   Let us pray together in the words our Saviour gave us:

All: Our Father . . .

C: Deliver us Lord from every evil, and grant us peace in our day. In your mercy keep us free from sin and deliver us from all anxiety as we wait in joyful hope for the coming of our Saviour Jesus Christ.

All: For the kingdom, the power and the glory are yours, now and forever. Amen.

C: Lord Jesus Christ you said to your apostles, I leave you peace, my peace I give to you. Look not on our sins, but on the faith of your church and grant us the peace and unity of your Kingdom where you live forever and ever. Amen.

Let us offer each other a sign of peace.

C: Let us thank God our Father for forgiveness.
All: God our Father thank you for forgiving me.
Help me to love others.
Help me to live as Jesus asked me to. Amen.

Dismissal
C: Go in peace to listen to God's call to build a better world.
All: Amen.

C: Go in peace to bring God's love to others.
All: Amen.

C: May almighty God bless you, the Father, and the Son and the Holy Spirit.
All: Amen.

Final Hymn: Make me a channel of your peace.

CHILDREN II (8-12 year's old)

Pierce Murphy

Hymn: We are sorry God.

Introduction
God our Father loves us. He loves us even when we are bold and do wrong. Like the loving Father in the Gospel he is always ready to forgive us. We come to him today to ask forgiveness. We promise him our love.

Prayer
Holy Spirit help us to see ourselves as God sees us. Help us to find out what we have done wrong. Help us to be sorry and give us the strength to live like Jesus.

Reader:
Jesus said: "Treat others as you would like them to treat you."

C: Jesus asks us to treat others well.
        When we hurt, insult, call names, ignore others we are not
        treating them well.
Have I treated my family and friends well?

Silence
C: Lord, have mercy.
℞   Lord have mercy.

Reader:
"Honour your Father and your Mother"

C: Jesus showed us how to honour and obey our parents. When
        we do not help our parents, disobey them or are disrespectful
        we do not honour them.
Have I honoured my parents and those in charge of me?

Silence

C: Christ, have mercy.

℞   Christ have mercy.

Reader:
Jesus said: "As long as you did this to one of the least of my brothers you did it to me."

C: Jesus invites us to be fair, to share and to be generous with others and to be friendly to all. When we steal, cause rows or do not share we are not doing as Jesus asks.

Have I been mean, selfish, jealous or dishonest?

Silence

C: Lord, have mercy.

℞   Lord have mercy.

Reader:
Jesus said: "I am not alone for the Father is always with me".

C: Jesus prayed to his Father every day.
         When we do not pray every day, rush our prayers, or use God's name outside of prayer then we are not with God and Jesus.

Have I skipped my prayers, used the name of God or Jesus when I should not?

Silence

C: Lord, have mercy.

℞   Lord have mercy.

Act of Sorrow
O my God I thank you for loving me. . .

C: Let us pray together as God's children:
         Our Father. . .

C: We give a sign to each other that we love and forgive each other.

Individual Confession

If individual Confession is omitted, the celebrant says the Absolution Prayer from Mass.

Conclusion

Prayer after Confession (together)

God Our Father thank you for forgiving me.
Help me to love others.
Help me to live as Jesus asked me to. Amen.

Prayer to the Holy Spirit (together)

Holy Spirit I want to do what is right.
Help me.
Holy Spirit I want to live like Jesus.
Guide me.
Holy Spirit I want to pray like Jesus.
Teach me.

C: We ask Mary to help us live as good followers of Jesus as we say:

Hail Mary. . .

C: May the blessing of God the Father, the Son and the Holy Spirit be with you always.
Go in peace to live like Jesus.

℞   Thanks be to God.

CHILDREN III

Sr Francesca Kelly

Theme: Happiness

Opening Hymn

Celebrant:
>   Peace and joy and happiness to all who gather here to ask forgiveness of their sins.
>   Peace be with you.

All: And also with you.

C: Come, Holy Spirit, and renew in our hearts the desire to follow the Lord Jesus.

All: Come, Holy Spirit, come.

C: God wants us to be happy and he also wants our friends to be happy.
>   Jesus was gentle with everyone and he wanted his friends to be gentle with each other. Then they would be happy and live in peace.
>>   'I leave you peace
>>   I give you my own kind of peace,'
>   he said to his special friends.
>>   'Do not be worried or upset,
>>   Do not be afraid.'
>   Today, the Lord gives us his peace, and he wants us not to be worried or upset or afraid. He wants us to be happy and he tells us how we can be happy.

Reading and Reflection   Mt 5:1-12
In the readings Jesus tells us what we must do to be happy and to live in peace.

Child 1: How happy you are, if you are poor!
>   God loves the poor! (Mt 5:3)

C:(i)   God wants you to know that you can be happy if you are trying to be good, kind and loving.

91

(ii) God wants you to be happy with what you have, and not to be looking for more, and more and more.

(iii) God wants you to share what you have with those who have not.

Child 2: How happy you are, if you are not very important! You are important to God! (Mt 5:4)

C:(i) God wants you to be patient, gentle and kind when others annoy you.

(ii) God wants you to keep silent when you feel like saying something mean.

(iii) God wants you to keep silent when you feel like answering back.

Child 3: How happy you are, when you are sad! God will comfort you. (Mt 5:5)

C: (i) God wants you to trust him when you are sad and lonely.

(ii) God will be with you when your friends do not want you.

(iii) God will help you when you are sad and feeling down.

Child 4: How happy you are, if you are keen to do what *God* wants! God will take care of you! (Mt 5:6)

C: (i) God wants you to treat others fairly.

(ii) God wants you to listen to your parents and to your teachers.

(iii) God wants you to pray — to speak to him each day.

Child 5: How happy you are, if you forgive others! God will forgive you! (Mt 5:7)

C: (i) God wants you to forgive when you feel hurt, and when it is not easy.

(ii) God wants you to forgive when others do mean things to you, on purpose.

(iii) God wants you to be kind and gentle to those who have hurt you.

Child 6: How happy you are, if you really want to know God! God will make sure you get to know him well! (Mt 5:8)

C: (i)   God wants you to be good and honest, and not look for praise for the good you do.

  (ii)   God wants you to be kind, not only to those who are kind to you.

  (iii)   God wants you to love, and not look for a reward.

Child 7: How happy you are, if you help people to be friends! God will be friends with you! (Mt 5:9)

C: (i)   God wants you to tell the truth.

  (ii)   God wants you to help others be friends.

  (iii)   God wants you to make friends as soon as a quarrel is over.

Child 8: How happy you are, if people attack you! Especially when you are trying to do what God wants! (Mt 5:10)

C: (i)   God wants you to do good even when others laugh at you.

  (ii)   God wants you to pray when others tell you 'it's stupid'.

  (iii)   God wants you to know that he will always be with you, when you are trying to do what he wants.

Examination of Conscience

C: We are happy when we do what God wants. Sometimes we do *not* do what God wants.

C: (i)   Are you satisfied with what you have, or do you look for more and more and more?

  (ii)   Are you willing to share, or were you greedy and selfish?

  (iii)   Are you gentle and kind when others annoy you, or do you say mean things and answer back?

  (iv)   Are you ready to listen to your parents and teacher, or do you give trouble at home and at school?

  (v)   Are you ready to forgive when you are hurt, or do you keep up a grudge?

(vi) Are you ready to be good and honest, or do you look for praise and reward for any good you have done.

(vii) Are you ready to help others be friends, and do you make up after a quarrel?

(viii) Are you ready to keep trying when others make fun of you, or do you feel ashamed and give up?

C: We have not done what God wants us to do.
We have not loved. We are sorry.
We confess that we have sinned.

All: I confess. . .

C: God our Father, we did not do what you wanted us to do. We ask you to listen to our prayer of sorrow.

All: O my God. . .

C: God our Father, we your children ask you to keep us in your love and care. Forgive us, as we say (or sing) the prayer that Jesus taught us:

All: Our Father. . .

Blessing

C: May God the Father be good to us, forgive us all that we have done wrong, and one day make us happy with him in our home in heaven.

All: Amen.

C: Go in peace to love God, to be happy yourselves, and to help others to be happy also.

All: Amen.

Hymn
A suitable known hymn.

CHRISTIAN UNITY

THE SPINNING TOP
Robin Boyd

Lord, we are so top-heavy — our whole structure
In session, Synod, Council and Assembly —
The whole thing topples, and to keep from falling
We, top-like, spin and spin on our own axis,
Self-centred, humming, whipped to static fury,
And so gyrating pride ourselves on action.

Lord, knock us sideways, send us spinning outwards;
Uncentre us from self, and make our axis
That transverse axle-tree, the Cross, that turning
On Christ alone we may roll forward, steady,
To that great day, when, every creature gospelled,
The End shall come, and nations see the glory.

Kohlapur, India, 1962.

CHRISTIAN UNITY I

Alan Falconer

This service is used with the permission of RTE radio who broadcast it in December 1980. The Service is conducted by a Protestant (CI:) and a Catholic (CII:) celebrant.

Invocation
Hymn or Psalm: *Theme: God's gifts of creation and of himself.*

CII: In the light of God's gifts to us, each of us is aware that we have failed to live as he intended, both in our individual lives and as communities. Therefore, let us offer our prayers of thanksgiving and confession to God:

CI: All glory, praise and honour to you, O God our Father,
   for creating us,
   for giving us the gifts of life and love,
   for daily nourishing us.

CII: All glory, praise and honour to you, Jesus Christ our Divine
      Redeemer
   for drawing us into oneness with yourself in the unity of the
      Father and the Spirit, through your cross and resurrection
   freeing us from bondage
   enabling us to live in liberty subject to no one
   enabling us to live in freedom subject and servant to all people.

CI: All glory, praise and honour to you, Spirit Divine,
   for enabling us to cry 'Abba' — Father
   for illuminating our minds and understanding
   for giving us the strength to love.

CII: We adore you, God, Father, Son and Holy Spirit.

CI: We acknowledge you to be Lord.
   (Pause)

CII: Lord, have mercy on us.
As Roman Catholics,
we have been slow to acknowledge the faith and love of members
of other Christian traditions; preferring to remain behind the
wall of separation; preferring to proclaim that outside our
boundaries there is no salvation; too often we have lived without
any reference to the members of other Christian traditions in
these islands; preferring to press for the implementation of our
needs — in matters of the family, education and the welfare of
society, we have been quick to point out the failures of others,
and slow to acknowledge our own inadequacies.
Lord have mercy on us.

(*Pause*)

May God forgive us our sins of omission and commission,
may he strengthen us by his Spirit,
may he keep us in eternal life
through Jesus Christ his Son, our Lord.

℟   Amen.

A prayer in similar tone from the Protestant celebrant follows here.

Hymn: *Theme: Glory to God.*

Readings
Eph 2:11-22

A reading from Paul's letter to the Ephesians.

You gentiles by birth — called "the uncircumcised" by the Jews, who
call themselves "the circumcised" (which refers to what men do to
their bodies) — remember what you were in the past. At that time
you were apart from Christ. You were foreigners and did not belong
to God's chosen people. You had no part in the convenants, which
were based on God's promises to his people, and you lived in this
world without hope and without God. But now, in union with Christ
Jesus, you who used to be far away have been brought near by the
sacrificial death of Christ. For Christ himself has brought us peace
by making Jews and Gentiles one people. With his own body he broke
down the wall that separated them and kept them enemies. He
abolished the Jewish Law with its commandments and rules, in order
to create out of the two races one new people in union with himself.

97

In this way making peace. By his death on the cross Christ destroyed their enmity; by means of the cross he united both races into one body and brought them back to God. So Christ came and preached the Good News of peace to all — to you Gentiles, who were far away from God, and to the Jews, who were near to him. It is through Christ that all of us, Jews and Gentiles, are able to come in the one Spirit into the presence of the Father.

So then, you Gentiles are not foreigners or strangers any longer; you are now fellow-citizens with God's people and members of the family of God. You, too, are built upon the foundation laid by the apostles and prophets, the cornerstone being Christ Jesus himself. He is the one who holds the whole building together and makes it grow into a sacred temple dedicated to the Lord. In union with him you too are being built together with all the others into a place where God lives through his Spirit.

Jn 1:1-5, 9-14

A reading from the holy Gospel according to John.

Before the world was created, the Word already existed; he was with God, and he was the same as God. From the very beginning the Word was with God. Through him God made all things; not one thing in all creation was made without him. The Word was the source of life, and this life brought light to mankind. The light shines in the darkness, and the darkness has never put it out.

God sent his messenger, a man named John, who came to tell people about the light, so that all should hear the message and believe. He himself was not the light; he came to tell about the light. This was the real light — the light that comes into the world and shines on all mankind.

The Word was in the world, and though God made the world through him, yet the world did not recognize him. He came in his own country, but his own people did not receive him. Some, however, did receive him and believed in him; so he gave them the right to become God's children. They did not become God's children by natural means, that is, by being born as the children of a human father; God himself was their Father.

The Word became a human being and, full of grace and truth, lived among us. We saw his glory, the glory which he received as the Father's only Son.

Here read the poem Child of Our Time *by Eavan Boland (*The War Horse, *Eavan Boland, London, Gollancz, 1975). The reference to the baby Aengus in the meditation which follows, comes from this poem.*

Hymn: *Theme: that we may be enabled to understand and appropriate the word of God through the Holy Spirit.*

Meditation
The text for our meditation this morning is from the passage read earlier from the letter to the Ephesians:

> "For Jesus is the peace between us, and has made the two into one and broken down the barrier which used to keep them apart. This was to create one single New Man in himself out of the two of them and, by restoring peace through the cross, to unite them both in a single Body and reconcile them with God" (*Alternative translation of Eph 2:14-15*)

Collect
May the words of my mouth and
the whisperings of our hearts
always find favour in your presence.
Lord God, our Rock — our Redeemer.
Amen.

This morning our meditation centres on two children. In their differing ways, the baby Aengus and the baby Jesus are a challenge to our priorities; to our ways of viewing ourselves; to our daily concerns. Both of these children ask of us the most searching and fundamental questions about life, its meaning and direction.

Aengus is dead — killed in May 1974 — because the differing communities in these island find it impossible to live together. Aengus is dead — because in these islands we are all so good at talking, but we find it very difficult to listen to anyone outside *our* culture, religious

99

tradition or economic group. He is dead — because of our lack of real commitment to trying to find a way in which every person might have the opportunity to enjoy the fullness of life. The baby Aengus now is a symbol of our failure. Despite the fact that he died in 1974; despite the fact that hundreds of other have been killed, maimed or destroyed as human beings, we have allowed time to pass — we have carried on not listening. We have allowed ourselves to be dominated by our own personal needs to make money, to gain a reputation or to care intensely only about our immediate families. We have seen no urgency in the needs of society.

As Christians, our responsibility and culpability is even more evident. We, who should have known better, have not risen to the challenge and opportunities presented. Within our different traditions, we have been so sure that we possess the truth. We have been so convinced that we are *the* saved and are in a right relationship to God that we have not sought nor expected to hear the challenge of the Gospel from beyond the walls and boundaries erected by our preconceived ideas. We have even gone so far as to label members of other Christian churches as either non-Christians, at worst, or less than Christian, at best. All of us have made of Christianity a rather private or personal affair: Christianity is about my salvation; it is about my relationship to God.

And so each of us has been happy to live with a caricature of other traditions. Each of us has been content with a caricature of Christianity. We have failed to take seriously the baby Jesus. We have failed to respond in faith and love to the One who was crucified precisely because he challenged the values, traditions and caricatures of various groups in the society of his day. He challenged the society of his day by his openness, his concern for others, particularly those who had been dismissed by the society of his day, those who had been killed because of a caricature — the lepers, the widows, the poor, the prisoners.

All of this demands our repentance; that is, it requires of us not just a readiness to confess our sins. It requires of us also a commitment to a New Life. But how can we affirm New Life in a situation as desperate as ours? Is not the message of Christmas precisely that New

Life is found in the most unexpected places? Does not the Gospel point us to the fact time and time again that it is in the midst of suffering, of hopelessness, of crisis that the birth of hope takes place? — that the vision of New Life emerges?

The Israel of Jesus' day was plagued by group rivalries, by economic imbalance, by distorted values. Israel as a nation was under the occupation of the Romans, in whose hands political power and control resided. There was no real contact between Romans and Jews except out of administrative or economic necessity. Each group resented the other: to the Romans, Jews were an uncivilised and uncultured people; to the Jews, the Romans were a military power who had no idea of what it was to serve God and to have an awareness of a Being more powerful than any human power, more just than any human system of justice.

Among the Jews themselves there was a variety of factions, each of which regarded itself as unique or exclusive for one reason or another. The Samaritans and the Jews had had intense rivalry for years — the Samaritans claimed a more direct line of succession to the first High Priest. So intense had this rivalry and hatred become that a group of Samaritans had strewn the bones of dead dogs in the inner sanctuary of the Temple on the night before one of the great Passover feasts, thus making it impossible for the Jews to celebrate their feast since the temple itself was ritually unclean. This had happened in the generation before Jesus and was in retaliation for the burning of the Samaritan temple by the Jews. Feelings still ran high between Samaritan and Jew.

Within the Jews there were also factions: the Essene community, a small monastic community, asserted that only by following their religious rule could salvation be acquired. The rivalry between the priests and the other religious was firmly established through questions of who had the best ancestry of priesthood, who were therefore closest to God, who were the best interpreters of the Law? The religious rivalries were also matched by economic groups. A large merchant class arose in Jerusalem which depended for its livelihood on the Court and on the Temple. Anyone who said anything against these institutions was attacking their livelihood. And a similar group of merchants arose in Caesarea to serve the Roman occupation. They looked with disdain on the poor backward folk in the provinces. Each group was only capable of asserting its own viewpoint. Each group was self-contained — it could learn nothing from anyone else. Indeed anyone who did listen to another group was suspect. It is not that people then were particularly evil. It is just that they had false priorities, as we can see in the light of Jesus. They were self-assured. They had defined themselves against others.

It is into this situation that Jesus was born. His whole life was a challenge to these priorities. His birth took place in economic squalor and his ministry was directed to the poor, the have-nots. His life and ministry invited people to transcend their preconceptions and their cherished convictions. He admired the faith of a Roman soldier; he spoke with a Samaritan; indeed a Samaritan figures as an example of how God would have us live in his most famous parable; he brought wholeness to lepers and to other physically and mentally handicapped people — normally outcasts of society; he gathered around him a group composed mainly of unsophisticated provincials; he questioned the priorities of the religious experts — theologians and churchmen — of his day. Ultimately he was crucified because he had transcended and challenged these self-assured divisions. In his own person he had shown forth God's peace, God's shalom, whereby God in his relationship with his people had brought wholeness. He had shown his people that his way was the way of inclusiveness and openness. This peace, so apparent in Jesus, was concerned with the whole of society, with every facet of its life — economic, political, social — and society was to be a reflection of God's care for us. It is for this reason that the Ephesian passage speaks of Jesus being the Peace between us, bringing hitherto alienated groups into unity in Jesus. This was a reality for the early church and is to be a reality for us. This peace is a reality for us in the baby Jesus. This peace is also our task today, not just so that Christians might enjoy the chumminess of such a life of wholeness, of living together. But so that they might be peacemakers. The German pastor, Dietrich Bonhoeffer, when he commented on the Beatitude, "How happy are the peacemakers", had this to say:

"The followers of Jesus have been called to peace, for when he called

102

them they found their peace, for he is their peace. But now they are told that they must not only have peace but make it. . . Now they are partners in Christ's work of reconciliation. They are called the sons of God as he is the Son of God.''

It is only by taking the birth of Jesus really seriously that we have any possibility of overcoming the deep divisions in our society. If we don't follow the openness and inclusiveness of Jesus, then we cause the deaths which Aengus symbolises. The challenge of the birth of Jesus, to the Christian and the churches, is to re-examine our priorities asking whether we are really prepared to love others in the costly way of Jesus — whether we are prepared to transcend our religious, political, economic and social groups, working for the well-being of our whole society.

May God give us all the strength for this task.
Amen.

CII: Let us reaffirm together our commitment to God by saying together The Apostles' Creed.

Hymn: *Theme: unity of the Church for the unity of humankind.*

Intercessions.

CII: God, Father, Son and Holy Spirit,
in this world of ours, of alienation and fragmentation, we pray for those who work for peace, who bring wholeness and healing, asking that you will strengthen us as we try to support them.

CI: For all working in medicine, whether dealing with the temporarily ill, the physically or mentally disabled, or the terminally ill.

CII: For all working among the marginalised in society — the travellers, the children sleeping rough, the refugees, the homeless.

CI: For all working in education, that the search for understanding and love may dominate them and through them inspire others.

103

CII: For all working in the media, that balanced reporting of events may help our society to face up to its own responsibilities for caring and sharing.

CI: For the agencies and agents of reconciliation, that their work might heal divisions between and within societies.

CII: O God, at this time, as we give you thanks for the birth of Jesus, the Prince of Peace, your Son, our Lord, who was born in poverty, who brought hope to people experiencing hopelessness, who dispelled fear through love and compassion, who gave wholeness and healing to all people, grant that we may be worthy to continue his work to the glory of your name.

CI: Grant to each of us as individuals, and to us as a community,
a pure heart that we may see you,
a humble heart that we may hear you,
a heart of love that we may serve you,
a heart of faith that we may always live in you,
and, with the saints of all ages and all places, enable us to say:

All: Our Father. . .

CII: As a symbol of reconciliation, let us offer each other a sign of peace.

Hymn: *Theme: Our service in the world.*

Final Blessing

104

CHRISTIAN UNITY II
Seán Collins OFM

Theme: The scandal of the disunity of Christians

It is envisaged that the gathering will take place in silence, or perhaps with muted instrumental music. Ministers do not enter in procession, but take their places singly and unobtrusively. When all is ready, a minister says:
(The participants stand, kneel and sit as considered appropriate)

Blessed is the Kingdom of the Father, and of the Son, and of the Holy Spirit, now and ever, and unto ages of ages.

All: Amen.

Two readers read the following, and the congregation answers each time:

Reader 1: My people, what have I done to you? How have I offended you? Answer me.

All: Holy God, Holy and Strong, Holy Immortal One, have mercy on us.

Reader 2: I came in love to Bethlehem to take you on my shoulders and carry you to Paradise: and you have preferred rejection and strife to peace and goodwill.

All: Holy God, Holy and Strong, Holy Immortal One, have mercy on us.

Reader 1: I went down into Jordan river with your sins upon me, that you might rise from the water of Baptism in innocence restored: and you fail to recognise my gift when given to another.

All: Holy God, Holy and Strong, Holy Immortal One, have mercy on us.

Reader 2: I went about doing good, with healing in my hands and comfort in my eyes: yet you avert your eyes from your own sister and brother.

All: Holy God, Holy and Strong, Holy Immortal One, have mercy on us.

Reader 2: I gathered you, my little flock, as the mother hen enfolds her chicks, and the shepherd his sheep and lambs: but you have spurned that enfolding, and gone astray.

All: Holy God, Holy and Strong, Holy Immortal One, have mercy on us.

Reader 1: I gave myself equally to all, in bread and cup poured out and shared: and even this, my precious gift, you made a sign of contradiction.

All: Holy God, Holy and Strong, Holy Immortal One, have mercy on us.

Reader 2: On Golgotha I died in ransom for your sins, that I might gather the scattered children of the Father: and you remain divided, O my people.

All: Holy God, Holy and Strong, Holy Immortal One, have mercy on us.

Reader 1: On the third day I arose in glory and breathed on you the Spirit of unity and pardon: yet you continue to grieve God's Holy Spirit.

All: Holy God, Holy and Strong, Holy Immortal One, have mercy on us.

Reader 2: Behold, I am with you all days, that you may be one as I and the Father are one, so that the world may believe: my people, hear my voice and follow me, that there may be one flock and one shepherd.

All: O Shepherd of Israel, hear us;
let your face shine on us
and we shall be saved.
Holy God, Holy and Strong, Holy Immortal One, have mercy on us.

A minister says:
Let us pray.
Almighty, ever-living God,
it is your will that in your beloved Son, Jesus Christ, all creation be made new and restored to joy.
Grant to us, your wayward children, such a lively awareness

of our failure to be Christ's co-workers in so great a task
that we may be seized by sorrow for what is past and urgency
for the work which lies ahead.
Rekindle in us, Gracious Lord,
that longing for unity and for the spread of the Gospel which
alone can erase the hurt of the past and harness all our
efforts, together, towards the coming of your Kingdom;
through Jesus Christ our Lord.

All: Amen.

All are invited to listen to God's Word.

First Lesson   Hos 12, 1-9
The tender love of our God will bend down to us once more, for we are his.

"Everything that the people of Israel do from morning to night is
useless and destructive. Treachery and acts of violence increase among
them. They make treaties with Assyria and do business with Egypt."

The Lord has an accusation to bring against the people of Judah; he
is also going to punish Israel for the way her people act. He will pay
them back for what they have done. Their ancestor Jacob struggled
with his twin brother Esau while the two of them were still in their
mother's womb; when Jacob grew up, he fought against God — he
fought against an angel and won. He wept and asked for a blessing.
And at Bethel God came to our ancestor Jacob and spoke with him.
This was the Lord God Almighty — the Lord is the name by which
he is to be worshipped. So now, descendants of Jacob, trust in your
God and return to him. Be loyal and just, and wait patiently for your
God to act.

The Lord says, "The people of Israel are as dishonest as the
Canaanites; they love to cheat their customers with false scales. 'We
are rich,' they say. 'We've made a fortune. And no one can accuse
us of getting rich dishonestly.' But I, the Lord your God who led
you out of Egypt, I will make you live in tents again, as you did when
I came to you in the desert."

Song
The *Song of Hosea* would be appropriate. Or any song of repentance and return.

Second Lesson   1 Cor 1, 10-17
The only source of our salvation is the Cross of Christ, beneath which we all stand.

By the authority of our Lord Jesus Christ I appeal to all of you, my brothers, to agree in what you say, so that there will be no divisions among you. Be completely united, with only one thought and one purpose. For some people from Chloe's family have told me quite plainly, my brothers, that there are quarrels among you. Let me put it this way: each one of you says something different. One says, "I follow Paul"; another, "I follow Apollos"; another, "I follow Peter"; and another, "I follow Christ." Christ has been divided into groups! Was it Paul who died on the cross for you? Were you baptised as Paul's disciples?

I thank God that I did not baptise any of you except Crispus and Gaius. No one can say, then, that you were baptised as my disciples. (Oh yes, I also baptised Stephanas and his family; but I can't remember whether I baptised anyone else.) Christ did not send me to baptise. He sent me to tell the Good News, and to tell it without using the language of human wisdom, in order to make sure that Christ's death on the cross is not robbed of its power.

Song
Any song which stresses the all-sufficiency of the love of God in Christ Jesus is appropriate, eg *For to those who love God*.

Third Lesson   Jn 15: 1-17
"I am the real vine, and my Father is the gardener. He breaks off every branch in me that does not bear fruit, and he prunes every branch that does bear fruit, so that it will be clean and bear more fruit. You have been made clean already by the teaching I have given you. Remain united to me, and I will remain united to you. A branch cannot bear fruit by itself; it can do so only if it remains in the vine. In the same way you cannot bear fruit unless you remain in me.

"I am the vine, and you are the branches. Whoever remains in me, and I in him, will bear much fruit; for you can do nothing without me. Whoever doesn't remain in me is thrown out like a branch and dries up; such branches are gathered up and thrown into the fire, where they are burnt. If you remain in me and my words remain in you, then you will ask for anything you wish, and you shall have it. My Father's glory is shown by your bearing much fruit; and in this way you become my disciples. I love you just as the Father loves me; remain in my love. If you obey my commands, you will remain in my love, just as I have obeyed my Father's commands and remain in his love.

"I have told you this so that my joy may be in you and that your joy may be complete. My commandment is this: love one another, just as I love you. The greatest love a person can have for his friends is to give his life for them. And you are my friends if you do what I command you. I do not call you servants any longer, because a servant does not know what his master is doing. Instead, I call you friends, because I have told you everything I have heard from my Father. You did not choose me; I chose you and appointed you to go and bear much fruit, the kind of fruit that endures. And so the Father will give you whatever you ask of him in my name. This, then, is what I command you: love one another.

One of the ministers gives the homily, or, depending on the size of the group, a shared reflection on the Word of God may take place.

Litany of Repentance
A minister (or cantor) reads or sings the litany, and all respond:

Minister: In peace, let us pray to the Lord.
All: Kyrie eleison *or* Lord, have mercy.

Minister: For the peace from above, and for our salvation, let us pray to the Lord. ℟

For the peace of the whole world and of all men and women everywhere, let us pray to the Lord. ℟

For the unity of Christians for whom Christ died, let us pray to the Lord. ℞

For the leaders of all the Churches, that they may have the courage to face the risk of misunderstanding in the quest for Christian unity, let us pray to the Lord. ℞

That we may put aside the bitter memory of past insult and scorn, and make room in our hearts for Christ's forgiving love, let us pray to the Lord. ℞

That the steadfastness of our forefathers in their religious convictions may inspire us to seek the truth God offers us now, even when accepting it costs us pain, let us pray to the Lord. ℞

That the Lord may preserve us from thinking that we alone have all the truth, let us pray to the Lord. ℞

That conflict and hatred which appeal to religion and breed on past wounds be banished like a plague from among us, let us pray to the Lord. ℞

That our children may inherit a faith which is strong and Christ-centred, and open in love to all his followers, let us pray to the Lord. ℞

That the dying prayer of Jesus, 'May all be one', may never be erased from our minds, and that we may never be guilty of delaying its fulfilment by thought, or word, or deed, let us pray to the Lord. ℞

That we may put aside our indifference and our pride, and begin to do all in our power to heal the scandal of our divisions, that the world may believe, let us pray to the Lord. ℞

Another Minister:
Therefore, let us commend ourselves, and one another, and our whole life to Christ our God:
All: To you, O Lord.

Minister 2:
For to you belong all glory, honour and worship, to the Father, and to the Son, and to the Holy Spirit, now and ever, and unto ages of ages.

All: Amen.

All keep silence for a time.

Then a minister leads a common confession:

Minister: God, our Father,
All: we confess that we have sinned against you,
and that we have failed to preserve
the unity of the Spirit
in the bond of peace.
We have not loved you with our whole heart.
We have allowed to remain fruitless
the power you have planted in us.
We have exhausted our energies in shallow rivalry,
and allowed our prejudice to blind us
to your presence in our brothers and sisters.
Forgive all that is past;
send forth anew your Holy Spirit upon us;
and bind us into a living fellowship
to the glory of your Holy Name,
through Jesus Christ our Lord. Amen.

Minister: As we repent of our failures in the past, we take hope from the unity we have already achieved. Let us listen to the picture of the church as she can be, proposed by representatives of all our Communities in the Lima Statement:

Reader: In a broken world, God calls the whole of humanity to become God's people. For this purpose God chose Israel and then spoke in a unique and decisive way in Jesus Christ, God's Son. . . The life of the Church is based on Christ's victory over the powers of evil and death, accomplished once for all. Christ offers forgiveness, invites to repentance and delivers from destruction. Through Christ, people are enabled to turn in praise to God and in service to their neighbours. In Christ they find the source of new life in freedom, mutual forgiveness and love. Through Christ their hearts and minds are directed to the consummation of the Kingdom where Christ's victory will become manifest and all things made new. God's purpose is that, in Christ, all people should share in this fellowship. The Church lives through the liberating and renewing power of the Holy Spirit. . . The Spirit calls people to faith, sanctifies them through many gifts, gives them strength to witness to the Gospel, and empowers them to serve in hope and love. The Spirit keeps the Church in the truth and guides it despite the frailty of its members. The Church is called to proclaim and prefigure the Kingdom of God. It accomplishes this by announcing the Gospel to the world and by its very existence as the body of Christ. . . The members of Christ's body are to struggle with the oppressed towards that freedom and dignity promised with the coming of the Kingdom. This mission needs to be carried out in varying political, social and cultural contexts. In order to fulfil this mission faithfully, they will seek relevant forms of witness and service in each situation. In so doing they bring to the world a foretaste of the joy and glory of God's kingdom.

Minister: As we look to the coming of the Kingdom, let us pray with one heart and one voice the words our Blessed Saviour gave us:

All: Our Father. . .

Minister: As a pledge of our earnest intent to pursue all that makes for peace and for mutual upbuilding, let us exchange a sign of peace.

The peace is exchanged in whatever manner seems appropriate.

Minister: And so to him who has the power to do so much more than we can ask or even conceive, to him be glory in the Church and in Christ Jesus, from generation to generation evermore.

All: Amen.

Minister: Go forth in peace.
All: In the Name of Christ. Amen.

A song of the mystery of the Church is sung, for example *Thy Hand O Lord has guided* (to Thornbury) or *The Church's One Foundation* (to Aurelia).

ON A PILGRIMAGE

To a Holy Well or local place of Pilgrimage.
To be adapted to local traditions and conditions.

Oliver Crilly

P In the name of the Father and of the Son and of the Holy Spirit.
℞ Amen.

Introduction

Opening Prayer

P Lord,
as we gather at _____ today
we thank you
for the faith of our people who have gone before us.
We thank you for the gifts you have given to each person here,
and especially for the people you have placed around us in our lives.
We pray, through the intercession of St _____,
for forgiveness for our sins
and for healing of all our hurts
and illnesses of mind and body.
We make our prayer with confidence
through Jesus Christ our Lord.
℞ Amen.

LITURGY OF THE WORD

First Reading   Rom 12:1-2, 9-19
A reading from the letter of St Paul to the Romans.
Be transformed by the renewal of your mind.
Think of God's mercy, my brothers, and worship him, I beg you,
in a way that is worthy of thinking beings, by offering your living
bodies as a holy sacrifice, truly pleasing to God. Do not model
yourselves on the behaviour of the world around you, but let your

behaviour change, modelled by your new mind. This is the only way to discover the will of God and know what is good, what it is that God wants, what is the perfect thing to do.

Do not let your love be a pretence, but sincerely prefer good to evil. Love each other as much as brothers should, and have a profound respect for each other. Work for the Lord with untiring effort and with great earnestness of spirit. If you have hope, this will make you cheerful. Do not give up if trials come; and keep on praying. If any of the saints are in need you must share with them; and you should make hospitality your special care.

Bless those who persecute you: never curse them, bless them. Rejoice with those who rejoice and be sad with those in sorrow. Treat everyone with equal kindness; never be condescending but make real friends with the poor.

This is the word of the Lord.

℞ Thanks be to God.

Responsorial Psalm   Ps 97:1-9

RESPONSE: The Lord has remembered his mercy.

Sing a new song to the Lord
for he has worked wonders.
His right hand and his holy arm
have brought salvation. ℞

The Lord has made known his salvation;
has shown his justice to the nations.
He has remembered his truth and love
for the house of Israel. ℞

All the ends of the earth have seen
the salvation of our God.
Shout to the Lord all the earth,
ring out your joy. ℞

Alleluia
Alleluia, alleluia,
Speak Lord, your servants are listening;

115

you have the words of eternal life.
Alleluia.

Gospel   Mk 12:28-34
A reading from the holy Gospel according to Mark.

One of the scribes who had listened to them debating and had observed how well Jesus had answered them, now came up and put a question to him, 'Which is the first of all the commandments?' Jesus replied, 'This is the first: Listen, Israel, the Lord our God is the one Lord, and you must love the Lord your God with all your heart, with all your soul, with all your mind and with all your strength. The second is this: You must love your neighbour as yourself. There is no commandment greater than these.' The scribe said to him, 'Well spoken, Master; what you have said is true: that he is one and there is no other. To love him with all your heart, with all your understanding and strength, and to love your neighbour as yourself, this is far more important than any holocaust or sacrifice.' Jesus, seeing how wisely he had spoken, said, 'You are not far from the kingdom of God.' And after that no one dared to question him any more.

This is the Gospel of the Lord.

℟ Praise to you, Lord Jesus Christ.

Homily
— life of the saint
— local associations and history
— symbolism (eg. water from the well, St Brigid's Cross, High Cross, monastic life etc.)
— saints are sinners who loved: we also are God's pilgrim people, weak, sinful, but trusting in God's love.

Prayer of the Faithful
P Let us pray to the Lord,
   who is enthroned
   on the praises of his people.
   Let us thank him for this place,
   for the life of St _____ and for this day.

Let us thank him for all our people
and for everyone gathered here,
remembering that thankfulness works miracles.

For everyone here present, for our families, and friends,
for those we particularly want to pray for,
that God will bless us all, through the intercession of St _____.
Lord hear us.

℞ Lord, graciously hear us.

We pray for the healing of physical illness,
that God's healing power may touch
all who are suffering in body, and heal them.
Lord hear us. ℞

For those suffering in mind or personality,
we pray that God will drive away all anguish, pain, hurt
    and depression,
and give them peace of mind and peace of soul.
Lord hear us. ℞

For the healing of relationships,
we pray that God will ease tensions in families
or between neighbours,
and that where there is hatred,
he may bring love.
Lord hear us.

℞ Lord graciously hear us.

Let us pause in silence so that each person may pray in the depths
of their hearts.

P Father,
    we offer all our prayers
    through the intercession of St _____
    and Our Lady and all the saints,
    and we offer them with confidence
    through Jesus Christ our Lord.

℞ Amen.

117

Litany of the Patron Saints of Ireland

Father in Heaven	Have mercy on us
Jesus Christ, redeemer of the world	Have mercy on us
Holy Spirit, our guide and consoler	Have mercy on us
Holy Trinity, one God	Have mercy on us
Mary conceived without sin	Intercede for us
Mary, assumed into Heaven	Intercede for us
Together with all sinners	we cry unto you, O Lord
Together with the sick and injured	"
Together with the lonely	"
Together with the heartbroken	"
Together with the bereaved	"
Together with the poor	"
Together with the oppressed	"
Together with the rejected	"
Together with the homeless	"
Together with the handicapped	"
Together with the unemployed	"
Together with all who are broken or maimed in spirit	"
In the name of all who are sad	"
In the name of all who are afraid	"
In the name of all who are angry	"
In the name of all who are joyful	"
That we may love and be loved as you prayed	"
That we may belong to one another as true disciples	"
That we may live responsibly in our relationships	"
That we may recognise the worth of everyone we meet	"
Together with Saint Patrick	"

Together with Saint Brigid   "
Together with Saint Colmcille   "
Together with Saint Malachy   "
Together with Saint Oliver Plunkett   "
Together with Saint Kevin   "
Together with Saint Laurence O'Toole   "
Together with Saint Ailbe   "
Together with Saint Jarlath   "
Together with Saint Mel   "
Together with Saint Macartan   "
Together with Saint Eugene   "
Together with Saint Mac Nissi   "
Together with Saint Colman   "
Together with Saint Felim   "
Together with Saint Finian   "
Together with Saint Eunan   "
Together with Saint Aidan   "
Together with Saint Conleth   "
Together with Saint Lazerian   "
Together with Saint Kieran   "
Together with Saint Colman   "
Together with Saint Finbarr   "
Together with Saint Fachtna   "
Together with Saint Brendan   "
Together with Saint Flannan   "
Together with Saint Munchin   "
Together with Saint Ita   "
Together with Saint Otteran   "
Together with Saint Carthage   "
Together with Saint Declan   "
Together with Saint Nathy   "
Together with Saint Attracta   "
Together with Saint Asicus   "
Together with Saint Colman   "
Together with Saint Fachanan   "
Together with Saint Muredach   "
Together with all the holy men and
women of Ireland   "

Let us pray
Lord, grant us the grace we need through the intercession of the saints
of Ireland. We rejoice to be their countrymen on earth. May we merit
to be their fellow-citizens in heaven.

We ask this through Christ our Lord.

℞ Amen.

THE SACRAMENT OF PENANCE

Preparation for Confession

P   My brothers and sisters, let us confess our sins and pray for each
    other, that we may be healed.

All: I confess to almighty God,
    and to you, my brothers and sisters,
    that I have sinned through my own fault
    in my thoughts and in my words,
    in what I have done,
    and in what I have failed to do;
    and I ask blessed Mary, ever virgin,
    all the angels and saints,
    and you, my brothers and sisters,
    to pray for me to the Lord our God.

P   Let us now pray to our Father
    in the words our Saviour gave us:

All: Our Father. . .

P   God our Father,
    we, your children,
    confess our sins and beg your forgiveness.
    Through the ministry of your Church, forgive us our sins,
    renew our Spirit
    that we may give you thanks and praise.

    We ask this through Jesus the Lord.

℞   Amen.

Individual Confession
The Rosary may be recited during individual Confession.

Prayer of thanksgiving
Father,
we thank you for the faith of our people.
We thank you for the traditions of penance and pilgrimage
which they have handed on to us.
We go through life as your pilgrim people.
Help us to accept the limitations we find in ourselves
and those around us.
May we always trust in your love and mercy.

We ask this through Jesus Christ our Lord.

℟ Amen.

Final Blessing
S Síocháin an Athar libh
   Síocháin Chríost libh,
   Síocháin an Spioraid libh.
   Gach lá agus oíche. Amen.

P Gach lá agus oíche. Amen.

S Coimirce an Athar oraibh,
   Coimirce Chríost oraibh,
   Coimirce an Spioraid oraibh,
   Gach lá agus oíche de bhur saol. Amen.

P Gach lá agus oíche de bhur saol. Amen.

S Beannacht an Spioraid oraibh,
   Beannacht Chríost oraibh,
   Beannacht an Spioraid oraibh,
   Go coróin na beatha síoraí. Amen.

P Go coróin na beatha síoraí. Amen.

S Bail ó Dhia oraibh
   ó Shamhain go lá 'le Bríde,
   ó Lá 'le Bríde go Bealtaine,

121

ó Bhealtaine go Lúnasa,
is ó Lúnasa go Samhain
is go mbeannaí Dia uilechumhachtach sibh, Athair, Mac ✠ agus
Spiorad Naomh.

P Amen.

S Go dté sibh slán faoi shíocháin Chríost.

P Amen.

or

P The peace of the Father,
Son and Holy Spirit,
be with you night and day. Amen.

May you be in the care of the
Father, Son and Holy Spirit,
every day and night
of your lives. Amen.

The blessing of the
Father, Son and Holy Spirit
be with you till you win eternal life. Amen.

And may almighty God
bless you,
the Father, Son and Holy Spirit. Amen.

Let us go
in the peace of Christ. Amen.

AT A WAKE

Andrew McCloskey

Where it is customary to have the Rosary late in the evening at a wake, this service could introduce confessions after the Rosary has been recited. Or it might be used at any time of the day according to local circumstances.

Sign of the Cross.

P The Lord be with you.

℞ And also with you.

Introduction

We are going to have confessions now for anyone who wants to take the opportunity of receiving the Sacrament, but first we will take a few minutes to prepare together. Let us listen to a short Scripture reading:

A reading from the book of Wisdom. Wis 3:1-9

They are in peace.

The souls of the virtuous are in the hands of God, no torment shall ever touch them. In the eyes of the unwise, they did appear to die; their going looked like a disaster, their leaving us, like annihilation; but they are in peace.

or

A reading from the Acts of the Apostles 10:36, 42-43

All who believe in Jesus will have their sins forgiven through his name.

'It is true, God sent his word to the people of Israel, and it was to them that the good news of peace was brought by Jesus Christ — but Jesus Christ is Lord of all men, and he has ordered us to proclaim this to his people and to tell them that God has appointed him to judge everyone, alive or dead. It is to him that all the prophets bear this witness: that all who believe in Jesus will have their sins forgiven through his name.'

This is the word of the Lord.

or

A reading from the holy Gospel according to John   11:21-27
I am the resurrection and the life.

Jesus said:
'I am the resurrection and the life.
If anyone believes in me, even though he dies he will live, and whoever
lives and believes in me will never die.

This is the Gospel of the Lord.

and/or

Responsorial Psalm   Ps 129

RESPONSE: Out of the depths, I cry to you, O Lord.

1. Out of the depths I cry to you, O Lord,
   Lord, hear my voice!
   O let your ears be attentive
   to the voice of my pleading. ℟

2. If you O Lord, should mark our guilt,
   Lord, who would survive?
   But with you is found forgiveness:
   for this we revere you. ℟

3. My soul is waiting for the Lord,
   I count on his word.
   My soul is longing for the Lord
   more than watchman for daybreak. ℟

4. Because with the Lord there is mercy
   and fullness of redemption,
   Israel indeed he will redeem
   from all its iniquity. ℟

A few words of reflection may be added:

— Death of a person causes us to reflect on our dependence on God
   and on his mercy.

— Where our dead brother/sister has gone, we too will have to go;
   our journey of life ends in death. Part of our journey is to seek
   reconciliation with God and with each other.

— Going to confession helps us to be prepared to participate fully in the Mass at the funeral, to receive communion, to unite our prayers with the family and friends who mourn. . . There is no more helpful thing we can do for them at this time.

Pause for brief examination of conscience.

All say:
I confess to almighty God,
and to you, my brothers and sisters,
that I have sinned through my own fault
in my thoughts and in my words,
in what I have done,
and in what I have failed to do;
and I ask blessed Mary, ever virgin,
all the angels and saints,
and you, my brothers and sisters,
to pray for me to the Lord our God.

All say together:
Our Father. . .

The priest concludes:
Let us pray.

Father, we thank you for your love and mercy.
Help us now to make a good confession, and forgive us all our sins.
Help us to live good lives that we may one day all be united in the kingdom of your love.

℞ Amen.

Individual Confessions now follow.